Intimacy with the Infinite

"Enlightenment is a destructive process. It has nothing to do with becoming better or being happier. Enlightenment is the crumbling away of untruth. It's seeing through the facade of pretense. It's the complete eradication of everything we imagined to be true."— Adyashanti

Intimacy with the Infinite

The Truth about Life after Awakening

By

Ananda Devi

Rasa Transmission International Books

San Diego, California

2019

Intimacy with the Infinite

The Truth About Life After Awakening

By

Ananda Devi

RasaTransmissionInternational.com

Rasa Transmission International Books
San Diego, California

This publication is presented to you for informational purposes only and is not a substitution for any professional advice. The contents herein are based on the views and opinions of the author.

What you do with this information is entirely your responsibility. If you do not agree with these terms, you may return this book for a full and prompt refund. Thank you.

Welcome to the RASA™ spiritual revolution with Ananda Devi and Ramaji!

Our unique one on one online coaching combined with RASA™ takes you step by step through the stages of awakening. In one year or less you can end your seeking and attain enlightenment (LOC 1000).

Subscribe to Our Monthly Newsletter:
https://www.rasatransmissioninternational.com/

Dedication

In life there are certain precious people who reach out and love in tangible and otherworldly ways. I am honored and deeply privileged to know these exceptional souls. These loving beings stood by me during a very dark, hard and confusing time in my life. They did not waiver. They loved me and they believed in me... even when I broke and fell apart. Their love and acceptance were instrumental in the writing of my book and in the telling of my story.

To my exquisite friend Sha, you are precious and special. You are a true treasure. Your consistent support, understanding and loyalty have been a pillar of strength for me that sustained me.

To my dearest Ron, meeting you and knowing you is a rare blessing. You are always there as a warm and true friend.

To my delightful and incredible Garyji, no words could ever describe how much you have helped me and truly been a constant support. You loved me from the second we met. Thank you.

To James, your talents, your generous love and your kind giving nature have been a unique and valued source of clarity during my time of need.

To dearest Jason, thank you for helping with our social media and spending your time with us. How you believed in me touched my heart. Your generosity kindness and loyalty have stood the test of time and distance. You are amazing.

To my Twin Flame, Ramaji, you are my angel and my better half. When I found you I found the love and the inspiration to be who I am. You cared, you nurtured, you listened and you believed in me. You are my miracle. I am eternally grateful and I adore you. No words will ever be enough to express the reverence, gratitude and the respect I feel toward you. You really are a master and a legend. In this lifetime we found each other. My truth and my heart are one with yours. You are my eternity.

To my beloved triplets, you are my heart and my inspiration. I admire you. I have the deepest respect for each of you. Being your mother has taught me more than I ever knew possible. My love is endless and unconditional. Thank you for forgiving me and thank you for choosing me. When I close my eyes at night, I see your faces and I know I have done something right.

This love I am is the force of the power of Truth. To live the force of love is the gift of my lifetime.

Butterfly

It was dark and I felt alone.

I stumbled off a steep cliff. The ground beneath me was nowhere to be seen.

I was submerged in my awareness. My body left behind. I was a single lost sparkle of electricity.

I felt bewitched and depleted. I did not believe I would ever land.

Enmeshed in the umbrage of my own dark cocoon, I felt the deepest yearnings. I was very confused.

Suddenly out of the blue I saw your scintillating Light. You were everywhere. Your radiance was dazzling. Your Light surrounded me.

You had a deep knowing smile upon your beautiful face. Your eyes sparkled with the wisdom of love and reverence.

You silently spoke those scintillating words to remind me.

"You can fly, my beloved butterfly! You have wings!"

Ananda Devi

Table of Contents

Foreword

You have in your hands a book like no other.

Ananda Devi is unique among modern spiritual teachers. She is that rare phenomenon of a total natural. She was born to do this!

This is the spiritual autobiography of an enlightened woman and mother.

She awakened spontaneously. She did not have a teacher.

She was surrounded by the trappings of wealth for most of her life. She gave up the substantial inheritance promised to her by her wealthy parents.

She is an Enneagram Eight. Very few Enneagram Eights become spiritual teachers or even show a serious interest in spiritual awakening.

Intimacy with the Intimate combines autobiography — the dramatic stories from her real life — with enlightened teachings based on the lessons of her post-awakening life.

Intimacy with the Intimate emphasizes the real truth about life *after* a deep spiritual awakening. This is the first non-duality book and first spiritual autobiography to focus on the post-awakening journey.

Ananda Devi walks her talk. She is the real deal. She is the most authentic human being I have ever met. I have known her for four years and she continues to amaze me, inspire me and teach me.

She is the most helpful and effective spiritual teacher that I know. If somebody was to ask me who they should go to, I would say go to her.

Our relationship is extraordinary. She blows my mind! I have to pinch myself because our relationship is a dream come true for me. Even the way she challenges me to grow is perfect.

As a loving woman and a mother, she brings that very special compassion and willingness to do whatever it takes to help her student awaken. If the student is sincere, she takes them on as her own, virtually guaranteeing their awakening.

Her voice is her own. She speaks from her heart based on her own experience. I think you will enjoy reading this very special book by a very special woman. You will probably feel the powerful impact of her Presence in these very pages.

Love, Ramaji

September 2019

San Diego, California

A Reluctant Mystic

I was a happy conventional spoiled housewife and mother from a wealthy family. When my spiritual awakening began to unfold in my life, my first reaction was to feel like a weird outcast. I experienced deep confusion as these opposing themes ran simultaneously in my already busy life.

The deep spiritual pull and various profound mystical experiences only increased my feelings of disorientation and hopelessness. I felt torn between my two worlds. Both worlds seemed equally real to me.

On the one hand I sincerely yearned to just be normal. Normal meant conventional. I love being a mother. I was completely fulfilled raising my triplets – two boys and one girl. I did not want my life to change!

I was raised by rich conventional conservative Jewish parents to be just like them. Spirituality, mysticism, meditation, intuition, psychic abilities, even talk of emotions and deep feelings, were seen as weakness.

I thought I was like them. But I wasn't.

I was embarrassed by the spiritual urges that had surfaced. All of that was "woo-woo" to me. I liked to think of myself as practical and realistic. That is how I was raised. I felt weird. I was misunderstood by my family and many of my friends. When I tried to share what I had learned they dismissed me and paid no attention.

In moments of unflinching self-honesty I knew deep in my heart that I was different. I knew that my two awakenings had shifted me yet I could not explain this shift. I felt depressed and lonely like never before.

A part of me just wished it had not happened. A part of me wanted to go back and only experience the comfortable old world. That old world felt safe.

My newfound Oneness felt odd and bizarre. Yet I knew that there was no going back. I was no longer able to lie or pretend. I felt totally phony if even a single word that was not honest and real came out of my mouth. I felt I had an important thing to do with my life. I didn't know what that was.

My role as a mother of triplets is huge for me. It is an important role I love. I just love being my children's mother. This led to deeply disturbing feelings. I kept on asking myself the same questions. Why me? What is going on? Why does my life have to change?

I asked even bigger questions. Do we have a say in our destiny? Do we know what life holds in store for us? Do we really have choices – or is choice itself just an illusion?

My spiritual awakening was not something I had yearned for or asked for! I had not been consciously seeking life-changing mystical events!

They just happened. A force took me over. This spiritual force within you and me has its own agenda. If it decides to take you over, you will be powerless against it. It took tremendous courage for me to accept it. It took a very long time for me to learn to go with it. It took me years to embrace completely what had happened.

In my case, I did not have a choice. I had to choose truth and live according to truth. Truth was pulling me in its direction. I fought it and resisted it with everything I had. It made no difference. The force of awakening and living in truth was overwhelming and unstoppable. I never had a chance!

My resistance to truth had been there under the surface of my life. The awakening revealed my resistance. I came to realize that this resistance was my opponent. You can see how you resist what is right in front of you.

What IS is right in front of you yet you still blindly resist it and fight with it. It took me years to understand how and why I was so fiercely resisting.

In order to lose my resistance, I had to lose my need to control. I had to stop demanding that things be the way I wanted them to be. I had to drop my need to control others and how they behaved. I had to let go of my need to be seen in a certain way in order to conform, be accepted and fit in.

Biggest of all I had to accept that I would never fit into my old box again. I had to accept that because I had changed many of my friends and loved ones had stopped wanting to associate with me.

I felt hurt, abandoned and deeply embarrassed by my mysticism. I tried to hide. I tried to continue pretending in order to fit in. In spite of all my efforts to pretend and belong, almost everyone I knew stopped communicating with me. It was so weird. I stopped bumping into the people that before I had regularly interacted with.

Now when I went food shopping for my family, I never ran into them! Or if they saw me, they did not recognize me or they totally ignored me.

Over a period of several years my whole world disintegrated in front of me. This total transformation of my life took place just as my tidal wave dream had predicted. It had warned me that a total destruction of my life was coming.

Nothing about these post-awakening changes was easy. The ongoing confusion and loneliness became unbearable. I was not able to stop whatever was happening. It happened whether I wanted it or not.

I could make no sense of it. Yet I learned to allow the people in my life to be the way they are and to love them anyway. I learned to accept them and let them be themselves. I let go of my demand for them to be the way I wanted them to be. This was my hardest lesson.

It was under these horrific conditions that I began to learn true unconditional love. When you can want for someone what they want for themselves that is unconditional love. When what you want for them is for them to do what you want them to do, that is control. That is not love! I had to learn the hard way. I made countless mistakes! I fought these lessons!

My lessons became so harsh and so extreme that they were impossible to miss. The obvious conclusion is that my narcissistic "little me" needed these drastic monumental experiences and life changes in order to really get it!

My reluctance and my resistance just kept on resurfacing. Why me? What the hell is going on? OMG?! Who is this?

To be honest, I yearned to return to the warm comfortable trance I had lived in. The pain of clear seeing was almost too much for me to bear. I liked shopping for shoes. I loved money. I relished feeling important because my father was important. I liked the feeling of being superior and the arrogant indifference that came with it. I even got off on my narcissism!

After my awakening, everything changed. Even though I still yearned for the ways of the past, none of it brought me joy anymore. I had seen through that.

As my reward for awakening, I was faced with all the inner crap that I had not wanted to face in myself. My own stuff felt like a giant mountain of intolerable garbage. My anger, my sadness, my judgments, my hatred for no reason, my arrogance, my need to control others, my spiritual bypassing... OH NO!

I learned that if you want to become current with your own true Self and your feelings in this life, if you really want to live as an awake being, you must address your own shadow issues. This is non-negotiable. There is no other path. Even people who are genuinely awakened can fall for this trap.

Clear seeing is required but just seeing clearly is not enough. Watching life is not enough. You must become engaged. You must discover how to FEEL with your whole body and with every fiber of your being. Through feeling you will discover just how full of shit you really are... even if you have awakened!

Can you use your inner ability to FEEL every feeling and acknowledge it and own it inside of yourself? Can you do this without fear? Can you do this without trying to suppress or control or deny your real feelings? Can you do this without lying to yourself? Can you face your own darkness?

There is nowhere to go! The real NOW is this total whole-body unblocked pure FEELING! Life is a mighty river. It is flowing through you right now!

This post-awakening phase was a nightmare for me. I was trained by my family to pretend. I was taught to not be vulnerable. I was taught that emotions are weakness. My own vulnerability was what I feared most. I had to endure years of seeing and clearing my fear, shame, anger and guilt.

In this process I did not just become angry. I became enraged! I discovered that thousands of false beliefs had been imposed on me by my parents, society and religion. I had been fed lie after lie. It was all lies!

My own belief systems and thought patterns became incredibly clear to me. I would sit in my pajamas day after day writing these false beliefs down on paper and then burn them. I have a fireplace in my living room. I burned page after page of my false limiting beliefs in that fireplace.

After weeks of doing this, of seeing, owning and burning my beliefs, I felt empty. I can remember the last belief that I burned up in my fireplace.

This one was the hardest for me to drop. Is God real? Is God just another belief? I knew the answer. Kill the Buddha. Kill God. Kill ALL beliefs!

This was an extraordinary time in my life. After I had ruthlessly burned up all my beliefs, an emptiness arrived as my new reality. It felt awesome!

I felt detached and grounded in my own source energy. My thoughts began to taper away into oblivion before I could finish thinking them. I stopped believing my own story. I began to paint and to write poetry.

It was a phase that I can only describe as pure being. Yet I felt numb. This surreal numbness engulfed me for two years. I still loved spending time with my kids. That has never changed.

If I was not with my kids then I was spending my time alone. I was happily absorbed in my newfound creativity. I had nothing to say. This was a good thing since I had no one in my life who wanted to listen to me.

Eventually my cloak of comfortable spiritual numbness began to wear thin. I began to see that this neutral emptiness was masking a deep aching loneliness. It had been a welcome break but now I had seen through it.

I became more and more aware of the loneliness. It grew and grew until I could no longer ignore it. This feeling of loneliness where nobody in my life cared about what I felt or what I had realized entered into my being with the force of a new tsunami. It was unwelcome but I had learned that resisting my feelings was futile. I was much less afraid of my feelings now.

When I accepted my feelings of loneliness a new feeling then showed up. I realized that I could do something about my loneliness! I could go out into the world and find an awakened person to discuss this new me with. This became my new motivation and determination. I had a new purpose! I felt inspired again!

I began to pray for my person! I would get down on my knees in my bathroom and pray for hours. Tears flowed from my eyes like crystal rivers.

I felt I truly *needed* to meet an authentic person – any authentic enlightened person – who could understand what had happened to me. I wanted to meet someone who would meet me where I am.

I knew I had spiritually awakened. I knew because I was no longer her. I was no longer my old small narcissistic self. Ironically, it turned out that the awakening was easy. Living as this awakened new Self was the hard part!

This new Self was very different. It was the irresistible force. It would take me over for the sake of truth. There was no point in fighting it. It was always right! I had learned to listen to it.

I could tell when my true Self was guiding me. In my case, though, my true Self didn't just guide me or inspire me. It would take me over completely. I would find myself taking actions that made no sense to me at the time.

This feeling universe in all its beauty and glory was only now opening itself up to me. I still had a world of feelings that I had not yet owned or integrated. There was still plenty for me to work through. I did not understand this back then. I did not know at all. But I vividly felt the Force.

When I embarked on my quest to find my authentic awakened person, I had no idea about what was about to erupt in my already bizarre and crazy life!

Insight

The Roar of Truth

"The greatest fear in the world is the opinion of others, and the moment you are unafraid of the crowd, you are no longer a sheep, you become a lion. A great roar arises in your heart, the roar of freedom."

— Osho

To live Truth is to live as you are and to know you are born to be and feel free. Freedom is truth. It is your nature!

How many of us say what we really mean?

How many of us do what we truly yearn to do with our lives?

How many of us suffer in silence afraid to claim our birthright as unique and special divine human beings because we are obsessed with fitting in?

Too many!

Awakening dissolves that inherent sheep mentality. That sheep mentality is the greatest distortion in our world today. To be who you are born to be is by definition living and being your Self.

It means you do what *feels* right. You spend time with people who are good for you. You wear the clothes that feel good on you. You say what arises in you just as you feel every feeling that comes up.

You are not resisting your own sense of being you. You express from your very core. You are an authentic human being. You are a precious irreplaceable part of the whole.

Consciousness is an intelligence that knows itself and experiences itself through YOU!

We cannot know our next thought. We certainly have no control over anyone else. Yet so many people live their lives consumed with their image. They hold back terrified of what may happen if they are just themselves.

The Truth loves and the Truth cares. It is inherent in the consciousness that is us. The supreme beauty is to recognize this ultimate PRESENT and to live IT as this NOW.

Anything in the way of Truth is by definition false. It has to go. This is the post-awakening process.

See and free your own Self from the invisible chains that have held you back. Being you is your birthright. Singing your song as a powerful and valuable person is your inheritance. This Roar of Truth awaits each seeker.

It is a rumbling that is always there below the surface. It is waiting for you.

That force is Truth. That force is Freedom.

It is YOU as you really are.

CLAIM it, BE it and LIVE it.

No one but you can do this work. The world needs you to roar your truth. The world needs your love.

The world needs you and you need you!

Wake Up *and ROAR*!

Ananda Devi

My name is Ananda Devi.

I am a flawed fighter for freedom and truth. I am also a mother and a spiritual teacher of non-duality.

My preferred style of teaching is called Zen. You have probably heard of it.

Of all the old traditions, Zen is what I resonate with the most. I love its directness and the no BS way the Zen masters transmit their message.

The truth is always simple. It must be lived. It cannot be taught. It is existential. This is my reason for loving Zen.

I am an Enneagram type Eight. For anyone not yet familiar with the wisdom of the Enneagram, an 8 is referred to as the Boss or the Challenger.

My nature is such that I abhor weakness — especially admitting to my own weakness! For most of my life I associated my rich inner world of emotions and feelings with weakness. This was a big error.

This tendency was massively exaggerated because I was raised in a family that prized intellect and indifference over feeling and caring. Their idea of emotional intelligence is to have no emotions at all!

As an Eight, it was already natural for me to hide my feelings and not talk about them. Even though it was not true of me at all, I pretended that I literally had no feelings! I managed to totally convince myself of this.

When it's not okay to ever talk about your feelings with your parents, this is a brilliant solution. As an Eight, I am naturally outgoing and talkative. By convincing myself that I had no emotions and ruthlessly suppressing them, I would have nothing deep or real to talk about.

Problem solved! I could pretend that life was wonderful... even if it wasn't.

Eights hide behind a tough and bossy exterior. Like Enneagram Nines and Ones, Eights always have anger lurking beneath the surface. On the plus side, I love to provoke and challenge. I cannot tolerate hypocrisy. My life's calling and my joyful triumph is when I can fight for the underdog and win.

It is rare for Eights to become spiritual — much less be a spiritual teacher! Life typically works for Eights. They usually end up on the top of the heap. They are not called the Boss for nothing!

I think it is especially hard being an Eight female today. Though I am very loving, quite feminine, love being a mother and like getting my nails and hair done like other women, I absolutely refuse to submit to anyone.

Please understand that it was incredibly hard for me to write this book. My pride is so great that it has been extremely humiliating. Writing this book and publishing the secrets of my life took a courage I did not know I had.

It took years. I would often have to stop writing. Because of my tendency to be tremendously private, at times the emotional pain was just too great.

My nature combined with my oppressive upbringing created the constant need to come across as bold, forceful and strong. It took years of looking at my blind spots to let go of my need to appear that way. I was raised to portray the perfect image of the perfect family.

Creating this persona was at the expense of my true Self. I had to be ground down to dust in order to shatter my Enneagram Eight "I am the boss" fixation. Undoing my fixation means that I can maximize the best of me and minimize the worst of me.

Did I mention that I can also come across as arrogant and full of myself? My arrogance hides my sensitivity and my empathy.

The simple truth is that you and I can never eliminate our fixation. Nor is that a desirable goal. It is the foundation of our personality. It is crucial to our humanity. But we can get to know our fixation extremely well.

This requires brutal and unflinching self-honesty. Then we can operate in the way that comes natural to us yet do so with wisdom, kindness and compassion. Each Enneagram type has its own way of being authentic and its own fixation to deal with.

My earliest memory as a little girl is my deep yearning to be given the approval and attention I craved. Then I could open up wide like a carefree bright yellow sunflower and shower my sweet innocent sunshine on everyone.

Instead I was raised by two powerful dominant controlling parents. As an Enneagram Eight, I naturally pushed back. It was automatic for me to be defiant often and loudly rebel against their attempts to control me.

Beneath my fierceness, I yearned desperately to be heard and understood. I was literally begging for someone to acknowledge my feelings and my sensitivity. I wanted to be seen and treated as an equal.

Instead, in order to insure my survival, I became what my parents wanted me to be. I became invulnerable and untouchable. I pretended all day to be someone I was not. I pretended that I was like them.

My Enneagram Eight need to feel powerful and strong and avoid my vulnerability at all costs fed into my unnatural performance. I was a world class actress. I could have won an Academy Award.

It was devastating for me as a teenage Eight to lose my innocence. I was always loyal. I learned that the world is a cold and dangerous place. I had to act as if everything was okay regardless of what I really felt. Due to my Eight fixation, this translated for me to always wanting to be seen by others as a strong person that no one can harm or hurt.

I cannot blame my parents for being overwhelmed and confused about how to handle me. Because I felt isolated and powerless, I rebelled whenever I could. These are feelings that Eights will fight against with all their might.

I generally felt inadequate due to the covertly critical way my family communicated with me. I often felt worthless and disrespected. In their eyes, I could never be good enough. I was bad and fundamentally flawed. This is how I felt when I expressed an opinion that was different from theirs.

As a teenager all I cared about was to feel and express my freedom. I could not tolerate being lectured at on how to look and behave.

Eights love attention. They will not back out of a fight if they believe in the cause. But as a teenager I could not win. I felt I had no way of really being heard, respected or validated for being myself.

An Eight will rebel when she feels controlled. She needs freedom. She abhors feeling dominated. The best way to completely alienate a teenage Eight is to control them by instilling fear in them.

This is what my parents did unconsciously. This parental style is awful and outdated. In my case it was enormously detrimental. The only way I could survive in their critical environment was to pretend I was somebody else. This error eventually led to the enormous repercussions that this book will describe.

I am extremely direct. I cannot tolerate phoniness and hypocrisy. I have a built in BS barometer. I cannot stand ambiguity, being ignored or any kind of spineless passive/aggressive treatment. But the worst form of torture for me is the silent treatment, a tactic my parents used against me when I stepped out of line.

Now I am in my 40s and I am the mother of triplets. I have one Enneagram Eight son and one Enneagram Six son. My daughter is an Enneagram Five. There is no telling them how to be!

Each of my children needs a different parenting style based on their unique Enneagram type. Thank God I learned about the Enneagram!

My biggest flaw is venting. I was able to pretend and hold back my inner storm for decades. These years of holding back, of not being honest and speaking my truth, took a tremendous toll on me. I felt that I had no choice but to act compliant and pretend to agree with those around me. I felt terrified of my parents.

My anger became tightly bottled up inside me. This led to chronic anxiety and depression during my teenage years. Years later, when in my forties I got divorced, I realized that I had been living every day of my life filled with irrational unexplainable fear and deeply embedded toxic shame.

The pattern became that every couple of years I would just lose it! I would write letters and texts that disclosed my hidden world of monstrous fury.

I could never do this face to face. I was too scared of my parents. The fear I felt was not normal.

These volcanic vents were the only way I could release my gargantuan inner tensions. My brother said that my style was to bring a gun to a knife fight.

When I met my life partner, he could see how scared I was inside. He soon realized that my wildly aggressive and irrational vents were the result of not being allowed to communicate my feelings freely as a child. He compared my anguished screams via email and text to a person shouting with bottomless frustration at a brick wall that would never listen.

I was never encouraged to be myself or to think for myself. I had blocked myself from knowing my own potential, talents, gifts and intelligence.

My life partner patiently taught me how to open up about my feelings and put them in words. He taught me to start sentences with the words "I feel..." My tendency as an Eight who was still unconscious of her Enneagram fixation was to be afraid of vulnerability.

Now that I had a good guide and a truly golden opportunity, I quickly learned how to reclaim my feeling self. We could communicate and finish the loop. We could talk it through instead of my bottling it up or venting.

This made a gigantic difference for me. It felt like a total miracle to be able to communicate like this!

I had always considered my passionate intensely feeling nature to be a terrible chronic fault. My family is incapable of dealing with real feelings. My opinions were viewed as dark and forbidden. I was never able to be who I am with them. Since I craved their love and approval, I took the blame.

My authenticity is foreign to them. They are not able to go there.

They never could and they never will!

My Eight nature is also naïve and innocent. Inside every Eight there is this hidden innocence. Their aggression protects it.

These toxic beliefs led to decades of blocking and suppressing my emotional body. When I did wake up to how much I had shut myself down, I had no choice but to suddenly feel all of my feelings without any brakes.

I was in for a shock. I had locked tons of emotional dynamite away in the dark depths of my being.

When my feelings were finally unleashed, I experienced an avalanche of incredible pain, fear, sadness, grief and rage.

It is only after years of recovery that I have reached this point where I can clearly see and own my Eight Challenger fixation. It is my blessing and it is my curse. Now that I know who I am, I am dedicated to being the best me that I can be.

I abhor coming across as a victim. This held me back from writing this book for a long time. I had to clearly see that I was pretending and not being real. I had to recognize my need to embody my truth. I had to find it in my heart to share my story in the hopes that my journey could help others.

I had to come clean!

I would have to expose about myself the very things I detest the most as an Enneagram Eight— my pain, my vulnerability, my innocence.

I realized I could not control how my readers would view me. Perhaps you will see me as a weak pathetic victim. Perhaps you will feel sorry for me.

This is a chance I have to take!

I want to help YOU, my beloved reader. That's why I wrote this book.

My healing required complete honesty. I had to expose with ruthless surgical accuracy what is true about me and what is false about me. No more acting. No more pretending. No more lying to myself or to others.

To do this is as frightening to me as jumping out of an airplane with no parachute! Maybe more so!

I want you to understand that I do not regard myself as a victim. If I can do it and overcome enormous obstacles, then you can do it too. I have painted the full spectrum of my drama in the brightest colors and the darkest shades so that you can take heart and be inspired to fiercely fight your own battles.

I take full and complete responsibility for my life, my actions and my story.

What I have learned is that true strength is the ability to be vulnerable. Now I know how to be strong in a way that is loving, tender and honest.

I want my vulnerability to help others feel comfortable with their vulnerability. Strength is always about being totally truthful and authentic.

Feelings are normal. They are not dark. They are not "bad." Feelings are a big part of what makes us human. Without them we become like robots.

Nothing is more important than to feel the feelings that spontaneously come over us. We can love our feelings as they are. We can encourage them to surface. For me, the richness of my feelings is what makes life worth living.

Our hearts soften when we express our truths and share our stories. Sharing allows us to heal and feel interconnected. We feel acknowledged and loved even with our perceived imperfections. This is the beauty of an authentic awakening. This is the power of love.

My journey has taught me to love my imperfections. I've learned to accept my faults, shortcomings and blind spots. I've discovered how to honor my emotions and feelings as being valid, legitimate and true to me. I'm a better person because I am acknowledging and owning my flaws.

I am a work in progress. We all are.

I sometimes talk about spiritual awakening as reaching the top of a high mountain only to look up and discover another even steeper peak that I will have to climb. We evolve because of our life challenges and our personal difficulties, not in spite of them.

I do not want to be done. I will never be done.

Climb I will, always, as long as I live!

Insight

Self-Deception and Spiritual Bypassing

"When you are sad, you should be completely involved in sadness without care for something happy. When you are happy, you should just enjoy the happiness."

— Shunryu Suzuki

One of the most frustrating misconceptions that I deal with as a teacher is the belief that lack of feeling is a sign of authentic spiritual awakening. This false belief has infiltrated many modern spiritual groups.

They believe that the highest state is to exist in a neutral blank state of no feeling. They think that if you act as if you are unaffected by life, attached to nothing and show no emotional reactions then you are spiritually advanced!

This is the most appalling pile of spiritual BS I have ever heard. Somehow this absurd and bizarre message that you will become an emotionless robot has reached many students around the world. They become confused into thinking that the sublime detachment and high indifference they seek will be a kind of comfortable numbness.

Nothing could be further from the truth. It is the opposite!

Authentic awakening is best described as living moment to moment in a state of unblocked feeling with your whole body. Feeling is wholeheartedly embraced. Feeling is not suppressed or denied. Feeling is celebrated!

Awakening is about getting in touch with truth and living that truth. It is about spontaneous aliveness as the truth. This path of true awakening is reflected in our increased ability to feel what is arising without blocks and without fear.

Society encourages us to live numb to our feelings. This numbness supports the global indifference which in turn perpetuates the abuse of innocent victims around the world. This blind neutral numbness is the problem that authentic real awakening rectifies.

We do not live in a thinking universe. We live in a feeling universe. We each have a totally unique personality. Our precious feelings are what unite us as a collective. Our ability to deeply feel is the foundation for our capacity to love and be interconnected.

It was only after my awakening that I discovered I was unconsciously using the spiritual concepts and beliefs that I had read or heard about to define and describe my truth. I saw that I had a habit of undervaluing my own existential now experience. I was clinging to ideas and concepts that had nothing to do with what was now going on with me.

I was trying to escape from this moment as it is. I was clinging to hope!

My mystical awakening was a profound blessing. It quickly dissolved that old spiritual habit. I then went on my authentic "real person" hunt. I wanted to meet at least one authentic human being who embodied this direct knowing.

I had no interest in objectifying, conceptualizing, dramatizing or even discussing the wordless. My interest was to live my truth fully.

This is the beauty of waking up. The world becomes a fresh existential experience. Each moment is unique and innocent. I feel everything. Feeling after feeling after feeling is experienced as a natural flowing river! The feelings flow through my body the way the blood flows through my veins.

"Resting in the absolute" is not a theory. It is not abstract. It is not a concept. It is obvious and you cannot exit the absolute even if you tried.

If you cannot be real with yourself then you are still missing the mark. The biblical meaning of the word "sin" in Aramaic is "to miss." You miss living your life when all you do is think about living without actually experiencing the now moment with all your being and with all of your capacity to feel.

It is just another trick to fantasize that you will become an avatar who is above human. It is just another false truth that freedom means you extinguish your very beautiful very human array of colorful emotions.

All this suppressing, missing and resisting is only another way to bullshit yourself. Ultimately you realize that the trickster is the mind and it will do whatever it can to remain in control. It is afraid of taking the backseat!

To die and be reborn may sound poetic but it is much easier fantasized than lived in its fullness. What is required is the annihilation of the false. This includes every single belief, concept, book, guru, teaching and teacher!

Then you can stand up and ROAR! Then you are no longer afraid of really living and truly being an authentic loving, vulnerable and real human being.

This will be the death of your false ideas about enlightenment. If you allow it, your true Self will arrange a string of events designed to kill the residue of falseness that persists even after awakening. This is deeply humbling.

This is the most humbling existential experience a person can have. You not only drop your residual echoes of false superiority, you drop your notions of false inferiority and even your false notions of being spiritual and enlightened!

Your lingering attachments to superiority, inferiority, spirituality, enlightenment and other false concepts are dropped organically. The you that survives this deepest of all purges is naked, fresh and innocent.

This is a new innocence that you have never experienced. It is a mature innocence that welcomes the other as your very own beloved Self.

This mature innocence enables you to live with ever deepening love and compassion. Your passion for truth has driven away anything that does not serve truth in all its glory. This truth that is revealed in each moment is your true face before you were born. You live happy, unconditioned and free.

Born an Empath

I always knew I had empathic qualities. I just had no clue to what degree. I recently researched the subject in depth. What I learned is that only 1 or 2 percent of the population are true empaths. While it is true that empathy is a trait shared by many in the human population, only a very small percentage are what can be called "deep empaths."

When you are a deep empath like me, it defines your life from the very start. It has taken me over 40 years to fully grasp the implications. My natural intuitive understanding feels like an instant download of wordless feelings. I am able to perceive directly with no intervening labels or ideas.

I feel what is really happening around me. In the past I thought that everyone must feel like I do. This is not the case. It is the opposite. Few feel as I feel. I realize now that I was always this way!

I've also realized that my belief that others must feel in the way I do set me up for profound mistakes in life. By assuming that others were empathic like me, I prepared the stage for my self-deception. I would project this onto my parents and others even when the evidence was very strongly contrary.

Paradoxically, I've somehow always known who and what I'm dealing with. I've often known things about the person talking to me that they themselves do not know. My brother called me "street wise" because of this ability to read people.

My parents did not notice this rare quality. If they did notice it was never mentioned. It was my life partner who picked up on how empathic I am. I was in denial. He picked up on it because he is a deep empath too.

I think my empathic radar did not work with my parents because my very survival depended on them. When empaths interlock with narcissists, the empath usually loses. The empath projects her goodness on the narcissist while the narcissist projects their negative shadow on the empath.

Once this exchange of shadows takes place, the empath is now stuck in a futile cycle of trying to help someone who does not want to be helped. This is deadly to the empath's happiness for she feels she cannot be happy until her loved one is happy. But her narcissist parent doesn't want to improve. All they want is to dump their shadow on another so that they never have to look at it, feel it or deal with it in any way.

There are a few stories from early childhood that demonstrate my deeply empathic nature. They are not my direct memories. My parents told me these stories.

In retrospect I've wondered why it did not occur to them that I was different? That perhaps I was different in a special good way? I do understand that most people do not operate at this heightened empathic level. My conclusion is that since my parents are not empaths themselves they must have chalked my behavior up to "kids do the strangest things."

Both my parents told me these stories. They were that unusual. There were no car seats back then. As a baby around 16 months old I had learned to open and close the windows by myself!

At this time in our lives my family and I lived in a very dangerous third world country. There were many homeless people walking the streets. These strangers would rush to the cars that had stopped at traffic lights to beg for money or food.

These poor people were often bare foot. They were tired, hungry and unwashed. Depending on the season, they were freezing or boiling hot. This country was the ultimate contrast between the rich and the poor.

The rich were oblivious and indifferent. The poor were not allowed to be educated or spend time on the beaches. These poverty stricken people had a curfew. To be honest, what I witnessed as a very young child is the greatest violation of human rights that I have ever been privy to or a part of.

To this day I feel deeply embarrassed to say I come from this strange, beautiful and dangerous place. I think that most people who were raised there must feel the guilt via association if they have any kind of empathy. Even though it was not my generation that created this social and economic catastrophe, our genes carry the burden. We carry the shame and guilt.

At 16 months I was a happy little baby. My parents called me a joy. Babies are without complication. They are not controlled by conditioned beliefs. They do not view the world as a grown up does. Babies see all equally without judgment or fear.

This is the nature of a pure consciousness. It is something we lose along our way when growing up. By some miracle a few of us remember how we were when we were uncorrupted.

We long to return there. Some of us are able to return. Usually this takes place only after years and years of seeking, of learning, of unlearning and of finally dissolving the whole thing! This return to Essence or our spontaneous natural self is called enlightenment. It is spiritual awakening into unity or non-duality.

I loved opening and closing windows in the back seat of the car. This was not something my mother appreciated! I would reach out and put my arms around the homeless people at my car window and exclaim "Kissy!"

I would hold them and kiss them. My mother would abruptly close the window. Then I would reopen it and continue on my hugging and kissing mission.

At some point I got the message and stopped doing it.

Another story was told to me by my father. This took place in Israel. I was 7 years old. It was a glorious summer day. My dad took me and my uncle to a popular flea market in our area.

Suddenly I started to act up. My father and uncle were extremely surprised. I was crying and moaning and screaming. I insisted that we leave. This odd behavior was uncharacteristic of me. They had no choice but to take me home. No matter what they said or did, I would not stop crying.

Later that day we heard the sad and painful news. A terrorist had detonated a bomb at the very same flea market. We had just been there! Many people were injured. Some had died.

My guess is that I felt something that warned me to get far away fast. As a child all I could do was cry and make a scene. The dangerous energy charge permeated the flea market causing me to panic and rightfully so.

I went to a public middle school. On my own initiative I would walk to a nearby old age home after school. I would visit with the elderly at least once or twice a week.

What I remember is that I loved sitting and talking and hanging out with these old people. Some of them did not have any family or friends. I really loved going to visit them.

At the time I had no idea that few young tweens do such a thing. But I didn't care what other people did. I was being myself! I was following my joy.

As a deep empath I was experiencing what I had always wanted to experience. I was giving love and that love was being received and given back to me. I was being appreciated and valued for my empathic gifts.

The circle was complete. I was starving for this kind of nurturing exchange!

Insight

Falling in Love with Presence

"Love is the bridge between you and everything."

— Rumi

The single most important factor during my awakening journey was my incredible knowing of my Presence. This Presence is often referred to as spacious awareness or as consciousness itself.

These big impressive words can be very misleading. I've found with my students that even long-time meditators may not be familiar with Presence. Even when they have spent many hours trying to be "aware of awareness," they still do not know Presence.

At first this Presence is experienced as just a background sensation. It is missed because it is always here. The spiritual seeker makes the mistake of looking for it in another place other than *right here* in this moment!

This pure open Presence is behind all your ideas, thoughts and concepts. It is the backdrop for the continuous story you tell yourself in your mind. It will be subtle at first. But it is your true home.

Post-awakening Presence is intensified to an astonishing degree. This silent backdrop becomes more and more real. It gets louder and louder. It intensifies itself until you can no longer ignore it. Even when circumstances are challenging, you feel your Presence strongly and clearly. It is obvious.

The unique unmistakable sensation of this Presence gets larger and more pronounced until finally Presence organically takes its place in the foreground. It becomes the most noticeable flavor or tone in your daily experience. Like the bright sun at noon, it dominates and permeates each of your moments.

This intense knowingness is there first always. But it is your habit to ignore it and take it for granted. This subtle and powerful Presence or pure open naturally friendly awareness makes all your experiences possible.

Your thoughts, feelings, body sensations and sense perceptions are possible only because of this background Presence. To awaken means to bring this glorious yet humble background Presence into your foreground until this sublime precious Presence is triumphant and dominates totally!

Until you discover Presence, what you truly are will be missed. Once you discover the sweet taste of your Presence, you will fall in love with it. After you fall in love with your Presence, your awakening is soon to follow!

When you awaken to your true Self or Presence it is a homecoming. It is a beautiful elegant knowingness that defies words. Yet it is audible too. It is a chord, a vibration, a tone. You can hear it as well as feel it. It is the sound of silence.

Presence begins to enhance itself more and more as you pay more attention to it. This is the power of spiritual integration. Colossal yet methodical, this switch from having your thoughts dominate in the front seat to having your thoughts sit quietly in the backseat is profound. It changes your life forever.

You discover that although this is your Presence you also share it with others. It has no boundaries. When this great switch takes place and Presence takes over you are met with Presence wherever you look. Everyone and everything share in this Presence. Everyone and everything are this Presence.

It is all the unbounded true Self. Deeply awakened people know this. They know that their Presence or true Self is the Presence or true Self of all. Yet paradoxically it is still your own unique individual Presence and real Self!

Most people are drowning in their stories. Most people are lost in words and concepts. They hear a concept like "spacious awareness" and then try to have an experience of it. Such concepts are at best helpful hints or pointers.

Please do not be misled by words or concepts. You are experiencing your Presence in this very moment. It is here right now as you read these words!

Presence is existential. Words cannot describe it. Even my meager attempt at describing the indescribable with my words must be taken with a very big grain of salt!

Your experience is the ultimate authority. This Presence is here right now. Do not go anywhere in your search to find it. Instead be aware of your sense of existing or your feeling of being and go right into it. Drop into it. Know it.

It will be your unique experience. It awaits every sincere spiritual seeker.

Presence is here now waiting for you. This is true every moment in every situation. Presence never leaves you. It is always with you.

Whenever you are ready, you will find your true home. It is here and now.

My Happy Childhood

My childhood was the happiest time of my life. My brother and I grew from children to teenagers before my father became extremely wealthy. We lived a basic middle-class life.

These years were full of love and fun. A cheerful atmosphere of optimism, enthusiasm and happiness was cemented via my father's upbeat personality. He is by nature an unflappable optimist.

I remember how I loved sitting on his lap. I remember driving in his beach buggy to various beaches in Israel where we would spend long lazy days on beautiful sun-drenched beaches. My brother and I would climb on big rocks and jump from those stone shelves into the freezing ocean!

I remember other days spent climbing trees with my brother. We loved to ride our bikes barefoot on the dirt roads outside our tiny flat.

I remember sitting high up on my father's shoulders and listening to his deep, contagious laugh. I remember the long fascinating stories he would tell us. I remember the delicious sandwiches he made. He took great pride in perfecting these yummy concoctions for us.

When my triplets were young children, my father helped me with the regular mom chores. He often picked up my kids from school. I will always be grateful to him for his hands-on help.

He has a certain innocence about him. I inherited that from him.

He is generous. I asked him to help a friend of mine whom was struggling financially. He did not hesitate. He gave me checks for her rent. He bought her grocery cash cards so that she could feed her family.

When I turned 15, he began to travel extensively. This was torture for me. I missed his big special energy!

As my father became wealthier and wealthier, I don't think he changed all that much. What did change was his availability. He was gone for weeks and months at a time. The business he is in requires lots of international travel.

Compared to the way it was when my father was around all the time, our home became very quiet. Without his infectious vitality bouncing off the walls, our family home became a silent empty house.

My mother was often unhappy when he was gone away on his business trips. Though there was little I could do, I felt responsible for my mother's happiness.

She changed a lot from his absence. I know she was very lonely. Maybe we all were but she took it the hardest.

Families that are suddenly separated feel it deeply. The long periods with my father gone had a strange psychological effect on me. I felt everything in our home had changed in unhealthy ways. Everything was different.

My parent's argument to justify his travel was money. My mother lectured us regularly on how our father was having to make great sacrifices so that our family could have our wealthy new upscale lifestyle.

A life of luxury, big houses and the best of everything! That's what my mother wanted – not me! These changes in circumstance felt insignificant to me although I did understand them theoretically.

I knew my father. I am a lot like him. He loved the power. He loved his job and the success it brought him. He was raised in poverty. But he was born to be a wealthy dominant leader of men.

My father thrives on being busy. He is never just doing nothing. He is constantly active in a state of high energy all day long. The only time he isn't in dynamic motion is when he is sleeping!

My teenage point of view was that my father had unknowingly made a deal with the devil. I knew instinctively that sharing personal face to face time and warm one to one presence is infinitely more valuable than *anything* that money can buy.

My father was not aware of how difficult it was when he was gone. He was oblivious. His main mistake was that he was not paying attention. He did not acknowledge what was happening.

I do not judge or blame my father. I will always adore the man.

I'm sure there are lots of teenagers who would not have minded his long absences. But I did. I didn't want luxury. I wanted my dad!

My brother and I did not ask our dad to do what he did.

We were already happy!

These were adult choices made by grownups. Kids are not extensions of their parents. They are born to be free beings.

Teenagers are supposed to find their own way and individuate. The gift we give our children is their independence. The ability to fly on their own power!

I was not raised to fly solo. I was raised to depend on my parents. I did not know better. I became my own person only late in life, in my 40s, as a result of my spiritual awakening.

My childhood memories are beautiful in their simplicity, purity and innocence. Unfortunately, when I finally stood up to my parents in my 40s and expressed my honest real thoughts and feelings plainly and directly for the first time as an adult, I didn't just lose my mother. I lost my father too.

Many things took place that led to my parents and my brother ceasing communication with me. Many nasty words were said to me.

I did not want to hurt my dad as his family was so important to him. I was devastated when he stopped communicating with me. He did not call, text or email me even on my birthday. He did not reach out to me or ask me what is wrong. I felt betrayed and hurt.

Words cannot express how the indifference of my parents and my brother hurt me. My father and mother broke my heart.

My father is a salt of the earth type of person. He is enthusiastic and full of life, but he does not have the emotional capacity to meet people with empathy and tune into where they are at. He lives blindly fully invested in his loyalty to his wife of 40+ years, my mother.

Just one month after I finally stood up for myself and asserted my truth after decades of deep devotion, loyalty and love, she totally cut off all communication with me! Yet for all those years, I had only been a kind, loving and devoted daughter.

My father, being blindly loyal to her, followed suit. Any pride I have in my family name is because of my father. I look like him. I walk like him. He was my role model. We have strikingly similar personalities.

At this time we are estranged. We do not have any contact with each other.

I have my father to thank for what I like about myself. I especially thank him for the strength, courage and abundant life force that has enabled me to not only endure the wholesale destruction of my life as I knew it... but to thrive now in my new liberated life because of it!

Insight

So What?

"Obstacles don't block the path. Obstacles are the path."

— Zen Proverb

Most who experience this unfathomable void just shut up! They do not talk or write about it because they know that no words can describe it. Not only that, whatever words you use will be misleading!

You can't describe this nothingness because there is nothing but it. Relativity in this groundless, spacious realm is non-existent. Nothing is nothing. When there is no one to describe the nothing because everything is this nothing the words are rendered totally pointless and meaningless.

Here is the secret the Zen masters are using all the way back to the beginning of time. They understand that the intellect is going to try to describe this phenomenon.

Though nothing compares to the void, our intellects are quite brilliant. Intellectuals get off on hearing their own voices drone on and on thinking that they can describe the indescribable.

A Zen master will happily knock you on the noggin or chop your head off. The master knows that your mind is trying to figure this out. He knows you are proudly flashing your impressive intellect in service of your small I.

To the master this small I which is everything to you is a totally irrelevant pseudo-entity worthy of utter destruction. The Zen master knows your attempts are acts of futility. She will send you back to sit in silence.

This silence is the best method to extinguish your hidden hopes. Yet this meditation in silence rarely invokes the actual existential experience. What it can do is show you the nature of your own mind. The master is amused at your impotent attempts to stop your unstoppable mind and its unceasing dialog.

A landmark session with one of my beloved students stands out as a good example. He had been an avid seeker for decades. He lived for several years in Burma as a Buddhist monk. This seeker went the whole nine yards!

After he had exhausted this monk experience he returned to the United States. He got married. He is now the father of two beautiful daughters.

When he first came to me he was at his wits end. He was desperate to awaken yet he knew that he could not do anything about it. He was finally at what I call "end of seeking."

He committed to having a session roughly every two weeks which is the ideal structure in my experience. It allows the student to absorb the session they just had yet keeps their awakening process on the front burner.

We had excellent chemistry and a similar sense of humor. We would go over his fears and doubt and whatever was confusing him the most at the time.

Like all of us, he had a tendency to get lost in his story. After working with me for a number of months, I intuitively felt his readiness for my Zen punch.

The session began with his usual complaints. After several more minutes of his moaning I spontaneously delivered the knockout blow.

"SO WHAT?" I thundered.

My words were met with silence.

Several seconds of shocked stillness ensued. I could sense his brain working overtime as it tried to regroup. His mind was reeling.

To my surprise, he began to laugh out loud!

He told me that after a long hard year of dedicated meditation as a monk in the Burmese monastery he had finally earned the opportunity to meet with the teacher face to face. Once a week he would sit on the floor in front of his Buddhist guru and talk about his fears, doubts and other issues. Every week the master would listen patiently and then send him back to sit in silent meditation.

This went on for weeks and weeks. He was once again agonizing over his self-centered never-ending story when the meditation master skewered him with a penetrating gaze. The master looked deep into the very core of his being and shouted...

"SO WHAT?"

Now, more than a decade later, he had received the same exact teaching!

He could not believe it. Here he was sitting in front of me on a computer screen via the Zoom video conferencing software and I had said *exactly* what his teacher had said back in the monastery. Not only that, I had delivered this mind-stopping message in precisely the same way.

Now he could hear it. Now he could absorb the message. Now he was ready. The teaching had not changed. The teaching was identical.

It is you, the student, who changes. It is said that when the student is ready, the teacher will appear.

What this really means is that when the student is emptied of his old views and is ready to wholeheartedly receive the teaching, the eternal teaching will appear in an effective form. There is no way to tell what that will look like.

Two years after my awakening I went on the road and met with several prominent spiritual teachers. I sought out the best. I was determined meet with them face to face and I did.

My meeting with Deepak Chopra stands out. Thanks to connections that my brother had, I was able to meet with Deepak for five minutes one on one over coffee. I needed only two minutes.

I had my question prepared. My reason for wanting to meet with Deepak was to ask him this specific question. We exchanged pleasantries. I had only minutes with him so I had to be as direct as possible. I dropped my bomb.

"Deepak, are we all dead?" I asked.

"We were never born!" he fired back.

His instantaneous reply was perfect. It was what I needed to hear and he knew it. That was my conversation with him!

I am impressed with Deepak. I know he is awake. I have no doubt at all.

He has the knowingness. His rapid direct response to my question might have appeared casual. But there was a boundless intensity in his eyes that impressed me beyond words. Those who know can see it in the others who share this marvelously ineffable intimacy with the infinite.

Pink World

My life partner was the first to recognize that I am a deep empath. Though I was born an empath, I was raised to not take my emotions seriously.

As a child, I instinctively created a solution to my difficult situation. I call it my "perfect love" pink projection. My pink projection of perfect pure love on my parents and on my brother enabled me to live in Pink World.

In Pink World love is everywhere and everybody is filled with love. This was the world I wanted to live in. So I created it!

Pink is my favorite color. As a little girl my father had always called me Pinky. It was one of my nicknames. I love it.

Being a deep empath, my natural inclination as an adult woman and later as a mother of three was to keep on making excuses for the cold indifference of people. In order to maintain my illusion of living in my perfect Pink World, I had to look the other way. In order to sustain my pink projection of their goodness and perfection, I had to take the blame.

I kept on telling my life partner that they did not mean it. I said "They are just acting out their pain and anger. I can feel their essence!" I felt I could internalize their Essence and somehow deal with their coldness that way.

The admission that my Pink World was not really working was the start of the radical unzipping of every projection I had ever made. Physical shock waves thundered through my body. I was overwhelmed by rage and fury. I was now seeing these people that I had loved unconditionally and painted pink for all my life as they really were! I was astonished by what I saw.

I was seeing them without my pink projection. It was a shock!

Empaths like me naturally see the world differently. We do this without trying. We have a rare and wonderful intuitive ability to tap into the underlying beauty in everyone. This is a beautiful gift, but it can be used to escape from reality.

My Pink World was a loving, safe and perfect place. I did not want to see my world otherwise. In the past, I could not see it any other way.

But this was all changing. After my spiritual awakening, my beautiful Pink World started falling apart. If the awakening is deep enough, spiritual freedom is inevitably followed by psychological freedom.

As a mother I see my children as perfect, decent and loving beings. Most parents will understand this. It is said that a mother's love is closest to the love of God. It is selfless. As mothers and as women we are designed to feel this way. This love is not a Pink World projection. It is real.

My childhood Pink World perspective reflected my need to view my family members in this way. My love was unconditional. I could only view my parents and brother as perfect, caring, sensitive, loving beings.

An empath automatically imagines that this love is shining itself on the whole world. There is an inability to be objective. This was not clear seeing. I was painting everybody, my parents and brother included, totally pink.

This was my Achilles heel. I would often argue with my life partner over my projections. I was refusing to see reality clearly!

The evidence had to build up to an extreme before I could finally let it go.

The pain and shock that followed was a real living nightmare for me. I became a stranger in a strange and frightening land. My Pink World became colorless and cold without my subconscious projection to fill it. The truth of what I saw without my pink paint was hard to accept.

It took a full year of mourning before I could accept it. Grief overwhelmed me as my pollyanna Pink World outlook was replaced by reality AS IT IS.

In the past, I would empathically and automatically do what I knew everyone around me needed. I was always feeling their needs as my own at the expense of my own needs.

I was now finally freeing myself of every projection. I was now able to find out who I was. Who is this real Self called Ananda? What did I stand for? What did I like? I had no clue!

Now, thanks to my awakening in my forties, I was finally going to find out!

One more thing. I remember where I came from. I came from a beautiful dimension where this pure perfect love is a reality. I came from a place that is the real Pink World.

When I came here to help my partner Ramaji, I came directly from there. To be honest, I didn't want to leave. It makes total sense to me now why I had so much trouble seeing this world as it is. I was used to living in a real Pink World where the love was real. It was all pure love!

Even though now I see this world as it is, I will never be able to understand how people can be so cold, cruel and indifferent to each other. Love is everything. Love is everyone. Love is the reality.

It is possible as people have done to narrow their consciousness and fight in the shadows. That does not make it real. They cannot see or feel the love but it is still there. My challenge has been learning how to navigate my relationships with people who do not see the world in the same way that I do... as a beautiful Pink World of pure perfect love.

Insight

Inject the Moment with Joy

"What the caterpillar calls the end of the world the master calls a butterfly."

— Richard Bach

A big part of awakening to Presence and living the truth is to become conscious of the vibration you are bringing to situations. The reverence and love that you feel when you are awakened is the electric injection of joyous Presence. It activates this Here/Now moment. It comes from inside of you.

You were taught from an early age that you are small. You may feel that you need to be saved by some outside force or by another person or by God.

No one saves us. We save God.

You save God when you can recognize Him/Her as a spark of your own Self. This humbling and dazzling brilliant Light lives in each and every particle of our universe. It lives in you as your Essence or Presence.

We are all a part of It. No one is left out. Owning your spiritual dazzle is a big part of living your realization. Essence or Presence surfaces during your awakening. It becomes clear and strong as you live courageously from it.

This post-awakening process takes years. It is like moving to a new city. At first everything is new. You feel lost. The newness of it all is fascinating and exciting but you don't have your bearings yet.

You know that now that you have made this big move there is still much to accomplish. You still need to discover where the grocery stores are and where the children will go to school. You have permanently moved but it is still going to take time for you to get fully acquainted with this new city.

The same applies when you move to a higher Level of Consciousness. When you move to LOC 1000 (Self-realization), the impact is massive. You live with a new perception of life and a radically new way of being you!

We tend to live our lives driving our car with our foot on the brake. Driving with the foot on the brake is an image for our habit of resistance.

As you awaken and your LOC gets clearer, you discharge your resistance. Your foot slowly and steadily lifts off the break. Eventually you are driving your car breezily down the freeway with no brakes.

You are free and enjoying your exquisite ride. Life just flows and there is no effort. There will still be twists and turns in the road. There will still be unexpected curves and bumps on your enlightened highway.

You do not know! Yet you do not care! You look forward to life's surprises!

Now you are driving with reverence and radiance. Driving is a joy. You are loving and relishing this extraordinary ride. Your life is one amazing trip!

Kabbalah Years

I woke up very early one summer morning. I was in my 30s. My family and I were on vacation.

My gynecologist had called me the day before. She wanted me to know that my yearly Pap smear had yielded an irregular result.

In that vividly surreal moment I awakened suddenly to my mortality.

My kids were much younger then. I felt afraid. I began to worry that I might have a serious life-threatening disease.

I got another test as soon as we returned. It came back normal. Even though I now had a clean bill of health, the knowledge of my mortality didn't go away. For the first time I felt I needed to find a teacher.

I had been a perpetual spiritual student and lonely seeker for many years. I had read a thousand books on a wide variety of spiritual subjects. In my studies of the world's religions, I had discovered the Kabbalah.

My contemplation of my mortality moved me to take action a few mornings later. After dropping my kids at school, an impulse arose to drive around in my local area. I was searching for something!

Suddenly I remembered a little storefront that was a type of bookstore. It was located near my family dentist. I had never actually entered the store before.

On this day, I decided to go in. That decision changed me and changed my life forever.

I picked a few books to buy. The topics fascinated me. I was riveted. Great excitement at the prospect of learning this study swept over me.

I asked the lady sitting at the front desk if I could meet the teacher of this Kabbalah Centre. She told me to call and schedule a session. In my arrogance I had assumed I could just walk in and see the teacher whenever I wanted.

My teacher turned out to be the lady sitting behind the front desk! She would be my teacher for the next two years.

I showed up for my appointment the following week. I realized that she was a truly beautiful human being. It was a revelation to look into her big brown eyes. They were filled with unconditional love. "I totally accept you just as you are." Her eyes spoke to a hunger that was deep in my soul.

She asked me a question. I started speaking. She tilted her head and listened to my every word. I felt I was witnessing a miracle.

She was listening to me and giving me her full attention. Nobody had ever really listened to me before!

Her gestures expressed a deep peace within her. The wholeness of her energy touched something dormant in my soul.

I felt a lump in my throat. I began to cry. I was overwhelmed by the love from this total stranger.

I realized that I did not know how to listen. This was the first of many lessons from her that were taught silently via experience, not words.

That same night I had a strange dream. A red-haired man dressed in jeans and a white T-shirt took my hand and started leading me somewhere.

I recognized him from the Kabbalah Centre. He had been in the store during my private session. I had met him very briefly.

He was very friendly. We were heading upwards but I did not know how we moving up. It felt as if we were floating upward together on a cloud.

I felt afraid. I started looking around for my family. I asked him if they could please come with us. I was concerned about leaving them behind.

He looked at me with kind soft eyes. "They are not ready yet. They cannot join you. Perhaps later... but not now!"

His response comforted me. I felt a load of bricks lift from my shoulders.

We continued upward. He was still holding my hand.

Then I entered a room. It had no walls. It was just a place.

Before me stood a big group of mystical sages. They did not look up. They were all praying. There was only peace there.

I felt like I had arrived at my true home. I did not feel scared or alone. I felt I was on familiar ground. I was just there with these elevated beings.

I sensed their sage-like nature. A feeling of deep reverence came over me. I had never felt feelings like this before.

This was when I woke up!

I felt this dream was symbolic. It was the sign to go ahead that I needed.

I knew from my dream that I had to learn all I could from my teacher.

These were amazing transformative years where I learned more about myself than I ever thought possible. An immense amount of knowledge and love was poured into me in a limitless unselfish way.

I think about my Kabbalah Centre teacher now I get tears in my eyes. I feel honored to have merited a single second in her presence.

My burning desire to learn and grow led to my mystical awakening years later. I was incredibly arrogant when I first showed up. They ground me down without mercy. I gladly submitted to their rigorous discipline.

I started purging my inner toxins. I began to see that the world and the people in my life are a mirror. For the first time in my life I began to take responsibility for my negativity, my judgments and my many other issues!

This understanding of my projections culminated in my mystical awakening. Thanks to this demanding Kabbalah training my vessel became prepared for the monumental events that were about to take place in my life.

I know now that it could not have happened otherwise. I am not a Kabbalah teacher. I am no longer involved with that center. Following my inner guidance, I eventually left and focused exclusively on my non-dual studies.

I do not regard myself to be at the heightened level of these sages. I would not ever regard myself as a true Kabbalist. I am in awe of them. I feel humbled to have learned from these deeply enlightened selfless beings.

Their love vibration is doing an enormous amount to regulate the imbalance we see in our world today. As a teacher I do my best to be an example just as my teacher was an example for me. I honor her by doing my best to share what I absorbed during my intensive training with her.

My goal with students is to honor them and praise them as the gurus they are. I help them claim their inner worth and their strength. I help them see their perfection and to love themselves unconditionally. Eventually that magic moment arrives where they recognize their individuality, their uniqueness and their true identity as their authentic Self or Essence.

When this astounding shift takes place in their inner lives and reflects itself in their outer reality, it blows my mind. I feel deeply honored to be a part of their lives. It is my great privilege to serve them and give them whatever I can in support of their awakening. This is the reason I do my work.

Insight

Turn Around Mirror Effect

"People seem not to see that their opinion of the world is also a confession of their character."

— Ralph Waldo Emerson

During my Kabbalah years I taught myself to always turn around. Using this simple turn around teaching I was able to see inside myself and own my own stuff. I did this for many years before I had my spiritual awakening.

I think this may be the reason I did have such a deep mystical awakening. My vessel had been prepared due to the years and years of hard work, of turning around. The turnaround is non-duality applied to everyday life.

Since it worked so well for me, I teach the turnaround to my students. You can use it too in your daily life. I think you will be amazed by the results.

This method presumes that you are deeply in touch with your feelings and your humanity. Many people choose to numb themselves out or live in their minds. They think that their detachment from emotion is a superior state. It is not. To be fully alive, a rich emotional life is essential.

The mirror effect is another way to describe the turnaround and how it works. In life you meet yourself in a thousand faces. Each person you interact with gives you a chance to reflect. When you have an emotional reaction to a person then you have a golden opportunity to connect with what you are creating within yourself.

When there is an emotional charge with another person it is pointing to your inner work. Sensing or feeling that you are being judged is a good example.

The feeling of being judged is very uncomfortable. This feeling points to your own inner judgment. If you were not already judging yourself internally then their opinion would not matter to you.

Or maybe you find that you are judging another person. The situation is the same. This feeling points to your own inner judgment. They are making you uncomfortable. You judge them and push them away in your mind.

The reaction is inside of you. Turn it around and you will see that you are judging yourself. The other person is a trigger for your uncomfortable feeling. But they are not the cause. The cause is your self-judgment.

We often project what we feel inside ourselves onto others. This habit of projection is so common in our lives that it typically goes unnoticed. Many of the biggest conflicts in the world are the result of unconscious projections.

It is extremely painful to see how judgmental *you* really are. It is a harsh reality that few of us are willing to face.

We are terrified by our own inner darkness or shadow. We desperately do not want to see it or feel it. It is so much easier and more comfortable to project our darkness outside of us and onto someone or something else.

This is a temporary solution to protect yourself from the excruciating pain of feeling and dealing with your own shadow, imperfections and flaws. In the long run taking this easy way out leads to hypocrisy and a closed heart.

Sometimes instead of projecting you introject. When you introject you take on another person's darkness hoping that you can help them heal themselves and feel better. This is what empaths like myself tend to do.

The empath believes that she can transform the other person by doing this. Based on my experience, I can say it rarely works out that way.

Yes, it can work when the other person is sincerely dedicated to working on themselves. My empathy plays a major role in my work with students.

The innocent empath believes that the magic of love will conquer all. She is forgetting the law of free will. If they don't want to awaken, there is nothing you can do. You must respect their choice to remain unconscious. Instead share your precious pearl of empathy with those who hunger for it.

With some of my family members, I would feel an inner darkness that really had nothing to do with me. I would hold and own the darkness for them in the hopes of lifting them into love and transforming them.

The big AHA for me was discovering how to distinguish between what is theirs and what is mine. I was taking on their shadows unconsciously. I suffered immensely and I could not figure out why. The answer was simple. I was owning their shadows but I was not acknowledging my own shadow!

Owning your own shadow, pain and discomfort is the way through. I know of no other way. Ignoring your shadow or projecting it onto others does not work. It only delays the inevitable. In order to free yourself you must become aware of the darkness in yourself, own it and make it conscious.

Life uses the turnaround or mirror effect to teach us via repeating events. Though the faces and places look different, when you turn around you see that these events all have the same emotional response or tone underlying them. Life will repeat this lesson until you learn it and integrate it.

You don't have to wait for life to hit you with a tough lesson. You can sit down right now, be quiet and reflect. Contemplate the themes that repeat themselves in your reality. Soon you will begin to see the common threads.

Turn around and face the problem. Be and feel the fear. Be and feel the anger. Be and feel the shame. Be it and feel it fully. This is the way through.

The only way to get past it is through it. This is how integration works. This work never ends. Before your awakening it is extremely important that you do this work.

After your awakening, you will need to do this work too. The difference is that now you will have tremendous clarity. You can access your inner darkness much more easily.

Paradoxically, after your awakening this turnaround work may get magnified. This is just in the post-awakening integration phase.

Although you will always be working on yourself, you do reach a point where your inner sky is clear, clean, open and beautiful. Dark skies are rare.

Awakening is about unity. It is about love and compassion. Self-absorbed narcissistic people with little or no empathy have no desire to do spiritual work. They do not believe they need it.

Yet they are the people who need it the most. They automatically project their inner darkness onto others. They pretend that they do not have a shadow. They totally deny it.

Because they live in their thoughts and avoid their feelings, they stay on the surface. Their relationships are not real. They do not know unconditional love. Their happiness is fragile and fleeting.

There is not a single person in the world that is let off the hook. To prepare for this liberation of love takes your conscious inner work. Not everyone will experience what I had to experience. The path is unique for each person.

When you resist and deny your pain and pretend that everything is happy when it is far from happy, you help to create immeasurable darkness. Yet the darkness, no matter how vast, begins to disappear as soon as the light of conscious awareness shines on it!

Spiritually awakened people are usually excited about doing this type of work. That you are eager to take on this challenge shows that you are ready for more growth. You and I are constantly are being called upon to expand.

This shadow work is the reason relationships can be so difficult. The fastest way to stretch and learn and evolve is through relationships. To be at peace secluded on a desert island or mountain top is easy. There is nothing wrong with going on a retreat, but it is in your relationships that you will be tested.

It is a lot more effective to jump all the way into your relationships. Practice the turnaround and don't hold back. Bring your consciousness of the mirror effect to a dynamic honest loving relationship.

Working on your shadow will happen naturally and you will experience a wonderful healing. Relationships are the ultimate spiritual retreat!

You will see that it is all relationship. There is no way to avoid relationship. It is seen that everything that comes your way is here to help you so that you can learn from your experiences and grow in love and wisdom.

Every single issue in life, whether it looks good, bad or ugly, is showing up in your life to serve your growth. Do the turnaround. Look for the mirror effect. You will see your inner shadow clearly. When you face your shadow and own it, your inner darkness shines. It turns out to be a great gold mine!

Intimate with the Infinite

When I was a teenager I had unusual sporadic episodes during my sleep. These sleep patterns took place as I began to fall asleep at night. I would remain totally aware in my sleep. Because I did not understand what was happening, it was extremely stressful and very scary for me.

I would spend hours wide awake yet fully asleep. It was as if I had left my body behind and I existed in a very dark, peaceful place. Believing that I was dead or dying, I would often fight this state and struggle to awaken.

I recently discovered that this phenomenon is called Sleep Paralysis. At that time, I was a teenager and I had no way of understanding what was happening to me. These experiences led to a chronic fear of falling asleep. I began to take sleeping pills in order to knock myself out.

My family is conservative and conventional. They are not spiritual people at all. I was raised Jewish and going to Jewish day schools while this was going on left me deeply confused about the nature of reality. Even so, I was fascinated with religion in all its forms.

In my inner being I became increasingly skeptical about religions. I clearly saw the hypocrisy that taints the various religions. I have always felt very connected to what some may call God. In my younger years, I simply could not believe that any true God could have a chosen people or be a strict punishing monster as is often depicted in Genesis.

Over the Jewish Holidays I would watch the more religious Jews fast, pray and try to absolve themselves from their perceived sins. Their behavior often continued being the same way after their fast. It was not something I could fathom as truth. It felt like a phony mess. I became determined to understand this apparent religious disaster that seemed to cause more damage on the world stage than anything else.

People fighting about whose God is the real God. Convinced that only their beliefs were true! That all other beliefs are false. Countries going to war and killing one another in the name of God. I could not and would not buy into it.

Eventually my sleep patterns became normal again without the meds. I got older but the memories are as vivid as ever. The feelings of peace, though laced with fear, are strong too. I was convinced I was not my body. Not my mind. Not my thoughts. These experiences were the catalyst to my seeking which would take place in earnest years later!

After these strange episodes of being awake while asleep I would then experience incredible feelings of bliss and joy. I felt like I was a light bulb. During my sleep I had been plugged into the source of electricity and the voltage. This voltage was so high and mighty that my whole body would arch in ecstasy. Though bizarre and strange, these feelings of bliss and joy after my episodes could last for hours even days.

Later I discovered that this kind of bliss is related to Kundalini awakening. As a teenager I had never heard of Kundalini. It was not anything I had any context for back then.

I never discussed any of this with anyone. I felt embarrassed. Also I was worried there may be something wrong with me. I wanted to just be a regular wild teenager!

Fast forward to my early 40s. I had learned all I could about the Kabbalah and other religions. I then met the man who convinced me to meditate.

I knew all about meditation by then but secretly I was afraid of it. I was scared because of my memories of my sleep paralysis. Somehow I knew that meditating would bring those experiences back in some form. I had decided to not go there. I was satisfied with my ongoing studies. I hoped that I could skip this part of my non-dual education.

When I met this man, it was one of these odd unexpected meetings where the universe gives you precisely what you need when you need it. I had become accustomed to noticing these symbolic events or synchronicities!

At that time, my children had a wonderful math tutor. It was a clear and sunny morning. I was wearing my workout clothes and dropping into my favorite coffee place to pick up my regular latte when I ran into their tutor. She introduced me to this man. He was her father.

This wonderful man took one look at me and began to cry! I felt confused yet there was a deep, knowing and kind look in his eyes. He was around 60 years old and extremely tall. His daughter was a warm and wonderful person. I was not surprised that her dad was kind and amazing too.

We became friends on the spot. He asked me a question that I was not expecting at all. "Do you meditate?" I replied that I did not. He persisted. "You need to start meditating!" I laughed and brushed him off.

I did not expose my fears about meditation to him. He did kindle my interest again. The serious way he said those words was fascinating. It was as if he really knew a secret. He was a good man, authentic and pure. I trusted him.

Our friendship centered around shared spiritual experiences and meditation. We went to the Self-Realization Fellowship to meditate together. We met in person a few times. We emailed each other. This phase lasted about a year.

Eventually he told me that he had had a dream in which his guru put his hand on my head. To my friend, this was an event of great significance. His guru had blessed me. It was an initiation to stimulate my enlightenment.

I remained the skeptic. Privately I dismissed his dream as woo-woo. A dream is just a dream! I really didn't think about it much after that.

In retrospect I would say that his dream had an enormous positive impact on me. It was the catalyst inspiring me and helping me to relax during my meditations. These meditations ultimately led to my spiritual awakening. Without his dream who knows what may have happened?

Another puzzle piece fell into place recently. I told Ramaji that my friend's guru was at the Vedanta Temple Society in Hollywood, California. It turned out that Ramaji had also gone regularly to that very same temple! This temple is dedicated to Ramakrishna and Divine Mother Kali Ma.

After a year of him begging me to start meditating, I finally listened. I took a Transcendental Meditation course. I liked the mantra approach. I was hoping that the mantra would keep me awake!

After I completed this five-day mantra course in meditation, I began to meditate at home. I would sit in my home theater. It was a soundproof room. I could dim the lights and make the room extremely dark.

It was perfect. I sat twice a day. First early in the morning and then after my family went to bed at night. It was winter. It was a cold February evening in 2014. I would wrap myself up in a robe and a blanket close my eyes and say my mantra. Thirty minutes would just speed by.

On the fifth day in the evening when everyone was fast asleep, I went into my meditation room. I began my usual mantra. Something unexpected happened. Suddenly I became bored with my mantra. I was tired of it. I don't know why. Spontaneously I switched to focusing on my breath.

After about half an hour I began to feel myself being pulled backward. I knew this feeling very well. It was the same feeling I used to get during my sleep paralysis episodes. I was terrified.

Before it could take me I forced myself back to waking consciousness and jumped up! My heart was pounding. I ran out of the room. I knew that the sleep paralysis that I dreaded was resurfacing. I felt terror. I was afraid of dying! I knew I did not want to go there! Where "there" was I did not know!

The next morning I called my friend. I expressed my fears and described what had taken place. I asked him for help.

He was extremely calm, almost as if he had expected this. He said "Do not quit. Next time relax and go where it takes you! You will not die!" His calming tone on the phone removed my fear. The way he said those words left me feeling comforted and confident. I vowed to let go and try again.

I decided right then that I had to somehow live through this obstacle and extinguish this fear. I knew that it was just a feeling. Plus I was becoming quite curious about it.

At this point I had read hundreds of books on non-duality. I had learned about the Void. I had studied non-duality in its fullness. This knowledge helped me relax when I started meditating again. I had no idea what was going to happen which would change my life forever.

I have often contemplated how one seemingly insignificant choice can change the entire course of your life journey. In my case, it was an unexpected meeting with a complete stranger. An apparently random yet fateful event like this can shift and change your reality completely.

The next evening I was in my home theatre again. Soon after I started to chant my mantra in my mind I felt the familiar relaxation. Before long I was totally relaxed. I didn't realize it but this was the first time I had forgotten to turn on my alarm that I used to keep my meditations to just 30 minutes.

It did not take long before my mantra dissolved effortlessly into the background. My breath came forward. I sensed a familiar rhythm as the breath flowed in and out of my body.

The room was dark and quiet. I was very still. I have no idea how long I was in this breath meditation phase.

Intuitively I welcomed the surreal and beautiful twilight time when you know you are falling asleep. I knew it and I allowed it. I felt my inner self fall backward. Far far far I fell back as my body relaxed ever more completely into deep sleep. I remained aware as my body's relaxation intensified.

Then it happened. I was out. Pop. Just like that, no thoughts and nothing to see. Pure spaciousness. I was nothing. I was fully aware that I was aware.

I was not afraid. I felt an inexplicable peace unlike anything I had ever known. I was still wide awake. I was still right here!

I stayed in this peace for what seemed like a very short time. I remember choosing to return to the waking state. It was a gentle desire to come back. I did not panic and try to jump out like I used to do.

When I looked at the clock I was stunned. I had been in that peace for the entire night. Eight hours had passed yet it felt like only a minute.

In a flash I realized what had happened! Now I knew who and what I am. I knew that this was the awakening people were talking and writing about.

This sudden knowing defied logic. This knowing was so deep and intense that it became my certainty. It changed me instantly and forever.

I could not think. I was incapable of talking about what had happened for days. The energy that was my deep Self had lit me up.

The colors of the world shined in hues I could not recognize. I spent days in my garden staring at this magical perfection. Oneness and nature merged in an extraordinary purity. Unconditional love took me over.

A bliss of enormous intensity rocked my being for weeks. I was not able to eat or sleep much. It was truly intoxicating. I could not function normally.

After a few days I was able to do my usual motherly chores but I was still in a trance. I did my duties but I was not there. I had discovered a reality hidden within my normal reality that was the same and yet so different.

I understood the eternal wordless truths and I was humbled. I felt overwhelming love, compassion and devotion for everything. Everyone I saw or spoke to was a God to me and a part of me. They were me. I did not think this. It was not a theoretical or intellectual understanding. It was cemented and concentrated. It was an inexplicable and complete knowing.

This magnificent state lasted for a full month. After the first week, even though I was still fully blissed out, my skepticism came back. I started to doubt my sanity. I made an appointment at my therapist. I also went to see two spiritual healers.

I was afraid. Suddenly I was convinced that I was bipolar and I was having a manic episode. My therapist told me I was normal and my mind was sound. The healers told me it was a spiritual breakthrough and I should be grateful.

The positive feedback should have comforted me. Instead I began to panic more and more. I started to feel that this love was too much. My body felt like it was exploding. Instinctively I knew I need to share it. It had to be released somehow or my body would spontaneously combust into flames.

This is when I took a tranquilizer. I could not tolerate any more! My vessel was not yet fully prepared.

Your vessel is also preparing for this Light. My vessel at that time was ill-prepared. I could only take so much.

I had known these truths before. Now I could recognize that this knowing and this level of consciousness and vibration are both there and right here always. At all times this is available to us.

This was my shift. This was my first awakening. I was instantly changed. The very fibers of my being were transformed. I felt changed completely.

I could no longer view my reality or those in it as I did before. My perception had shifted so dramatically and so significantly that I was a new me.

I was reborn. On the outside I was still married and the mother of three tall smart teenagers. I was still a conventional housewife with wealthy Jewish parents who lived just minutes away in the same upscale gated community.

On the inside I had gone through a transmutation. I had been a skeptical conservative caterpillar. Now I was a butterfly. Now I was unrecognizable.

At the time I did not grasp how revolutionary my transformation was. Nor was there any way for me to know ahead of time that a radical total purge was about to take place in my life.

It would take me years to figure it out. None of the hundreds of non-duality and enlightenment books had prepared me for this massive life-changing event or its consequences.

My motivation in writing this book is to inform you so that you can be prepared. Awakening is different for everybody. In my case spiritual awakening was destructive to a staggering degree. Unthinkable incomprehensible horrific change was about to take place.

Everything that was false fell away. What I did not realize at the time was just how thoroughly false my life was. When the false fell away as it does after a genuine enlightenment event, my entire life fell apart.

My life was a house of cards built on shifting sands. So much of what I had thought was true turned out just to be my imagination. Almost all of it was my projection. I was in for the shock of my life.

My tidal wave dream announced all of this. I could not have asked for a more clear warning. It came just months after my first awakening.

Insight

The Void

"Concentrate on the Seer, not on the seen. All that you see is false and the Seer alone is true."

— Ramana Maharshi

I am aware of the limitation of words. Yet I must write about the unfathomable void. That cataclysmic encounter was the ultimate and most impactful of my mystical experiences.

I had no idea how acute, penetrating and stupefying this void episode would be. It was also incredibly disturbing. It was an indescribable dive into an electric voltage of nothingness. This plunge into the deepest of deep ends was followed by an immense knowing that consumed everything.

The void devoured me whole. Everything I thought I knew or believed was annihilated in an instant. This spiritual extinction event accompanied my first awakening in 2014. It then triggered the events I describe in this book.

Here is the essence of what I want to say: at the end of the day your I AM is not really here. It does not exist at all. Non-duality refers to this as awareness aware of itself as nothing. I cannot improve on that statement.

A full encounter with the void or nothingness is a systematic unfolding of an unlimited knowingness that is unalterable and irreversible. It deconstructed, reconstructed and reengineered my entire world view.

There is no more speculation. There are no more questions and above all there is the collapse of any desire to speak. This massive shift rendered me utterly speechless.

My experience is that after a deep awakening in which there has been this life-changing encounter with the void, post-awakening notions of arrogance, elitism or any other kind of "Look at me... I'm special... I'm enlightened!" will quickly fall away. Now that you know with certainty that your individual I AM is created from this absolute nothing and is none other than this infinite nothingness there simply is no basis for such comical posturing. To heavily invest in hubristic positions after knowing the void approaches the absurd.

Prior to this titanic event I had believed that I was a little me. I was convinced of this. After this astonishing void event took place the little me was consumed and devoured by the changeless, unlimited, serene darkness of nothing at all.

Here is the fascinating part. Although I now know that my I AM spiritual spark or soul is not really here and that ultimately it does not exist, in the end I did not lose my sense of I AM.

There was no need for that. Losing my I AM would have meant loss of being able to function with this body. I would not be answering to my name. This mindless state has no value. Life wants you and me to be our unique I AM.

The existential import was that I now knew the real truth about I AM. I now knew that what I AM and who I AM is not what I think I AM. My I AM had dissolved into the void yet that did not mean it had to die a forever death. Instead it was seen that I am this nothingness *and* I am this totally unique exquisitely individual delightfully personal I AM at the same time!

This clear seeing enables me to live both as that unlimited nothingness and as this playful personal I AM at the same time. This I AM is indivisibly one with infinity. Therefore, the ultimate truth is I AM THAT.

This certainty or knowing of the absolute nothingness is macabre in how it radically confirms the death into and rebirth as the inscrutable oneness that mystics speak of. The need to be separate as a little individual is consumed in the emancipating fire. This divine fire then spits you out to be a unique dynamic version of itself. The wisdom of space dances carefree as this I AM.

My little me was seen through with inscrutable clarity. I was terrified and gobsmacked by this ruthless bald-faced knowingness. It took years for me to digest this internally. It took me years to adjust my personality accordingly and return to normal functioning. On the outside I appeared to be the same but on the inside a wholesale destruction followed by a total regeneration took place.

When all we know is separation and all we see is the illusion and all we believe is that everything is somehow separate from everything else… to suddenly without warning become aware of the infinite true Self as absolutely nothing and everything is a traumatic shock bigger than the biggest earthquake. I was convinced that I was totally alone. I was convinced for a while that I was actually dead!

As big and bizarre as this was, I knew that it was all me somehow. My entire nervous system was reprogrammed by this astonishing revolutionary clarity.

I was horrified and yet ecstatic all at once. Why does no one talk about this?

I recognized that this nothing is pure energy. It is alive. It is totally aware. I had taken for granted my experience of separation. I loved being separate. I enjoyed my individuality. I loved my old life as my little me too.

I enjoyed being an arrogant Enneagram Eight filled with a sense of my own personal power! I have felt powerful since the day I was born. Yet claiming the power of the infinite to be your own is the great Eight mistake.

I have concluded after years of contemplation that the ultimate is consumed with delight at being able to have the unique experience of thinking and believing that it is an individual. It separates in order to enjoy the return to its oneness and its fullness and its nothingness.

It wants to have its cake and eat it too!

This day and every day I bask in the non-dual knowing of nothingness which translates experientially into the profound pleasure of being an individual too. The clarity of being able to be both fully and completely all at once is the final peace and the joy. The freedom is in the duality as well as the non-duality.

It is not one or the other. It is both yet it is neither!

My Tidal Wave Dream

I was fast asleep! It was the middle of the night. It was spring, 2014.

I was standing in my family's holiday home. It was a bright beautiful sunny day. I could hear the ocean. Crashing waves were the backdrop.

I knew I was having a dream. I was fully aware of the fact that I was asleep. At the same time I could see and feel myself as a character in my dream. I felt I was being split. One part of me was the dream character. The other part of me was just calmly aware.

As the dream character I was overseas in my family's vacation home in our home country. I had not visited there in 15 years. It was one of my favorite places in the world. I felt a comfortable certainty that everything is okay. I felt a deep warm security being in my familiar family surroundings.

I noticed my dad standing next to the fax machine talking on the phone. He was working. He worked all the time. Even on vacations. He was waiting for documents on his fax.

Next I noticed my brother. He was straight ahead of me in the kitchen. He was wearing a bathing suit and making a sandwich. I watched him make his sandwich. He looked relaxed yet preoccupied.

Suddenly I knew that something ominous was about to happen. I turned my gaze toward the glittering ocean. I saw it. The biggest tidal wave I had ever seen. It was almost to our balcony. It was a gigantic wave. It seemed to reach up to the sun.

I felt calm and serene. I remembered that I was watching. I took refuge in that surreal knowledge. It was at that moment that my father and my brother noticed the wave!

I felt their terror and panic. Where was my mother? Asleep? We did not know. Soon their panic filled the living room like a mammoth crowd of crazy people. My dad was screaming. He was trying to gain control!

He ordered us to get out. He grabbed my brother. They rushed toward the door. "We need to get to the top of this building!" he screamed.

I was trying desperately to calm them down. "Stop! Stop!" I shouted. "It's too late!" I knew there was no way we would escape our pending death. Even if we managed to get to the top of the building, the massive tidal wave was too big. It would annihilate the entire city!

"Please don't be scared," I pleaded. "Please be calm. You cannot die. We cannot die!"

I did my best to stop them from panicking. Their fear enveloped me like a thick mist. I was suffocating from their panic.

"Relax. We can't die." How I wished they would listen! I turned around just in time to see the wave hit!

I woke up in a sweat. I was safe in my bed. It was the middle of the night. My husband was sleeping next to me. I knew my kids were safe in their beds and fast asleep.

I sensed that my dramatic dream was a premonition but I didn't want to listen to it. I dismissed the dream as a nightmare. I continued to have mixed feelings about my dream. I couldn't get rid of my feeling that this dream was prophetic.

I remained confused about the dream until the enormous changes it had predicted began to come true in a series of huge unexpected life events. As the dream predicted, I would be hit by life impacts the size of tidal waves. Just like in the dream, they caught me totally by surprise.

Soon after that dream my life became a series of tidal waves. There were more dreams, signs, synchronicities and symbolic events. I started paying attention to them. I learned to never ignore my inner voice.

This dream had warned me in advance just how enormous and shocking the changes ahead would be. A tidal wave of that magnitude would destroy everything in its path. In 2016 the message of my tidal wave dream began to be fulfilled. My old life was destroyed.

Why?

Because of love.

Insight

Post-Awakening Confusion

"The tree that would grow to heaven must send its roots to hell."

— Friedrich Nietzsche

Many spiritual seekers have unrealistic expectations of awakening. For example, they may think that becoming awakened means that they will no longer be human beings. They may believe that they will never have thoughts again. They may believe that they will no longer have emotions.

I have heard so many misconceptions about awakening from students that I cannot list them all here. Another misconception of seekers is they believe that they will not be affected by life's colorful array of issues. Another false idea is that the awakened person won't have to work to earn money. Money will magically appear.

The reality is that awakening is simply the permanent recognition of the big Self as you. You are still able to think. You still have a personality. You still have an Enneagram fixation. You still operate as a human being. In fact you are now more human than ever before.

That you actually become more real and authentic as a human being after your awakening is a great paradox. It is humbling to be aware of your feelings and your vulnerability. Our feelings unite us as a collective being.

We still have families to look after. We still work for a living. The irony is that seekers hope to escape reality. They hope to "transcend" and become "above human."

After your awakening you will know that there is no escape. There is nowhere to go. This is it. This right now. Just as it is.

In awakened individuals the desire to escape fades away. Your big Self is now running the show, not your mind. The big Self is now always in the forefront. You develop certainty that this pure Beingness is you.

This knowingness gives you the certainty that regardless of appearances life as it is now is going to work out best for you. You have intuitive certainty that regardless of what seems to be happening it is for your highest good.

The need to control an uncontrollable existence drops away. You stabilize in the natural state. Natural means natural. It is not high. It is not low. It is not bliss. It is not love. It is sahaja. Natural. Effortless. You are the flow of life.

It takes time to fully integrate sahaja and start living that way every day. In the beginning some people complain and moan that their awakening is not what they expected. They ask themselves questions like "Why am I thinking? What is wrong with me? Maybe I'm not awakened?"

This doubt is an old habit. The old habits of the mind do not go away right away. Your fixation is not gone. You still have a little I. You need your ego to survive. You cannot exist on this plane without a body and ego.

The difference is that now you know you *are* the infinite big Self and as the big Self you *have* a small self who helps you function as a person in life.

The best advice I can give you if you are going through this phase of post-awakening is challenge your mind. Your mind is full of shit. It talks like it knows what is going on but it really doesn't.

Do not allow yourself the luxury of believing a single thought. Who believes this? Dive into the belief. Who feels this way? Dive into the feeling.

Intense negative emotions are like tornados. Go into the heart or core of the emotional tornado. Who is there? Is there anybody there?

Please understand that post-awakening the mind still believes there is a real entity, a real "me" or "I," that its thoughts or emotions are all about. You must educate your mind and show it that there is NOBODY at the center of the tornado. The center of the tornado is open and empty. Nobody is home!

Repeated often this existential investigation will extinguish your doubts. If you persist in showing the mind that in reality there is no one there, it will eventually accept the evidence and stop its protests.

The feeling of having a personality and operating as a certain Enneagram type or fixation will remain. The difference is that your *knowing* has shifted. You no longer believe those old programs. That is what they are – programs.

You now operate spontaneously from a higher place. You are able to use your personality and your ego to serve the highest good.

The nature of your mind is to think and to doubt. Using the mind for everything in life is one of our old habits. This is a conditioned idea.

When you are planning a trip or doing math are good times to use the mind. When you are writing or doing something that requires thoughts, the thoughts just come and go. We use the mind. The mind does not use us.

Feeling takes over. In order to live in this intuitive genuine effortless way, you make your new habit to feel it all. Live in feeling and feel everything. Eventually the mind will give up. It will move to the backseat of your life vehicle which is where it belongs. Thought is no longer needed for living.

Your mind is a tool for creation. Use it for positive manifestation. It is not you. It is only your tool. Use it wisely. You are the master. It is the slave.

Second Awakening: Dropping into the Heart

On a gorgeous summer day in 2014 I decided to go on a hike. I love hiking and there are many trails near where I live. I love being outside in nature.

I went alone. I was very familiar with the territory. I had hiked this trail many times. I decided to not take my dog Benji with me. It was too hot for my furry friend!

I hiked to a special spot that is surrounded by graceful trees, rugged rocks and purple flowers. I decided to walk downhill to a small hidden river that only a few locals know about. As is typical for me, I walked with a fast pace.

I had to stop when I noticed that the shoelace on my white Nike running shoes had untied itself. I bent down to retie my shoelace. It happened on my way back up.

As my body stood up, I felt my heart *drop*!

I don't know how to describe the sensation.

It was a massive drop. It was immediately followed by a gigantic explosion in my chest. It was where my heart is located but it wasn't on my left or right. It was my whole chest.

My heart had blown open!

The blast went out in all directions from my body. It exploded out from the front, sides and back of my body.

I was instantly enveloped in a state of such total boundless love that I can only describe it as surreal. The immense power of this love felt like a miracle.

I had felt an overwhelming unconditional love with my first awakening earlier in 2014. This was at a whole new level. This love was so infinite, so perfect, so total that it seemed impossible and unreal.

After what seemed like just a few minutes of being in this frenzied love madness, I began to feel very dizzy. I had to sit down. Instinctively I put my hand on my heart. I was paralyzed into silence and fell into a deep trance that lasted for hours.

I was in a beatific state of indescribable bliss. There was only perfection and an inner knowing of this perfection as unconditional intoxicating love and light. The energy inside of me and the energy outside of me merged.

This magical unification transcended and transformed my usual internal and external way of experiencing. Everything was now literally LOVE. There was not one thing that was not made of love. It was all love. All of it!

If only I could explain this! Love had become my only experience. Love was now reality itself. Loving and being loved had disappeared. Love was reality!

Words are not possible. It was not romantic love or parental love. It was not any kind of human love. It surpassed human love the way the sun surpasses a light bulb. There was no comparison.

It was a love that exists only in another realm! For reasons unknown I was dramatically introduced to this exquisite celestial level of consciousness on that special day.

All I could do was remain still and bask in this ultimate knowing. The entire universe had become this amazing love. This love-bliss was reality.

My astonishment continued unabated. I felt that my being was being blown up like a massive balloon. I was this ever expanding balloon. I wanted and needed to pop! My heart ached intensely from this brilliant ecstasy.

I don't know how long I sat there. I had arrived at the spot in late morning. It was now late afternoon. Time had stood still. I was too overwhelmed and entranced to care. I was utterly consumed by this love-bliss fire.

These hours had seemed like minutes. Now that I was returning to my senses, I noticed that the painful ache in my chest was getting deeper and stronger.

My thinking process reasserted itself. Am I having a heart attack? Is this cardiac arrest? The heart pain felt physical and real.

I managed to pull my body back up. I found my way back to my car. I drove home. I could not think clearly on my drive back. I didn't know what had happened. I had no idea what to make of this experience.

When I got home I did not try to express what had just happened to me to anyone. I laid down on the big cream sofa in my living room. I returned to this amazing realm of heavenly love-bliss and got lost in it again.

Understanding this sublime, potent and bewildering dimension was beyond me. It was invisible yet its reality was without question. Somehow my consciousness had tapped into it. It was the most unusual, unthinkable and incomprehensible experience of my life.

It was so bewildering and beautiful that it was almost too much. Well into that evening I was still marveling. I was still feeling the heartache in my chest but my fear had slipped away. I had been lifted to paradise, a paradise that I now knew was real right now in this very world.

Fortunately, I had read a few books that described this kind of mystical love-bliss experience. I was amazed by how accurate and close to my experience these descriptions were.

Skeptical by nature, I had assumed that the authors were exaggerating. I need to personally experience something before I can believe it.

They were not exaggerating! This surreal super-real celestial love-bliss dimension is impossible to describe. You cannot do it justice. Any attempt to use words or to talk about it is doomed to failure.

After hours of allowing myself to relax, just be and get lost in this realm, the chest pain subsided. The actual feelings of love and bliss were a constant for about six weeks after this initial event.

Just to be sure, I went to my doctor and insisted on a cardio test. The chest pain from my heart blowing open had felt very physical. I wanted to rule out a possible heart attack. The test proved that my physical heart was fine.

This experience is always fresh in my being. It was an unforgettable experience so magical and so astounding that it made a permanent mark on me and my life. As I write this, I can remember that feeling but I cannot call it back with full intensity.

I think the lesson for me is that it is one thing to experience this infinite perfect love and recognize that it is everything and everyone. To live that truth as a human being is a different kind of challenge.

It is humbling to realize that no matter how hard I try I will never fully express this ultimate love dimension. I will keep trying for the rest of my life but I will never be able to fully share it or embody this love without limit.

I now know with absolute certainty that this Love, this Light, this Energy, this God-like vibration, is us. The unique intelligence that we call our Essence is also this unconditional love. It is now crystal clear to me that this boundless unconditional love is the energy that sustains this universe. This amazing indescribable love actually IS everything!

Another ongoing theme is preparing my vessel. As remarkable as my experience was, it showed that my vessel was not prepared for that much Light. I had been able to access that level of consciousness but I could not live it day to day.

I believe that this dimension is where each of us is headed if we are doing our spiritual work. I also believe that I merited this ultimate surreal love experience so that I can be a messenger who announces and shares this stunning realm. I am here to say that it is real. I am here to say it is possible for each of us and it is possible for humanity.

This vision motivates me to do my own work on myself and encourage my students to always do their inner work. I do my work and they do their work. Together we are preparing for the exciting and magnificent next phase of our evolution as human beings and as a planet.

Insight

Consciousness, Unity and Compassion

"So then, the relationship of self to other is the complete realization that loving yourself is impossible without loving everything defined as other than yourself."

— Alan Watts

When the spiritual seeker discovers Presence it is always a beautiful recognition. It does not stop there. Post-awakening there is a further step in which the heart opens completely.

This dropping into the heart enables your awakening to fully blossom. It is the key to post-awakening embodiment and integration. It may take some time before this dropping into the heart takes place, but it is part and parcel of a real awakening.

Presence is not an abstraction. It is recognized via feeling. The nature of consciousness as us gets reflected and mirrored back to us in all that we see. For this reflection to be fully appreciated, the heart must be open.

This seeing of unity when the heart is open naturally produces a sense of deep compassion. You now know that you share this one Consciousness or Presence or Self with everyone and everything.

Some students get confused because their existential experience post-awakening is not suffused with peace, love and compassion. Integration means integration of body, heart and mind. This cannot be taught.

External events may need to take place post-awakening in order to deepen and solidify your awakening. This takes time.

Compassion and consciousness are intertwined. They are two sides of the same coin. One is essentially a part of the other.

Via the full recognition of this unbounded richness that we all share your awakening transcends ideas like problem and conflict. This universal truth is seen to be so incredible and amazing that the mind surrenders.

Awareness infused with love solves the idea of being a separate little I. It is seen that even this small I is itself purely and totally this wonderful fusion.

Only form makes us seem separate. We are all interconnected.

Consciousness is filtered via your body and your personality. Awakening clears your consciousness so that you can know consciousness as it is. Your experience of consciousness is no longer compromised. Then body and personality are enjoyed as valuable and enjoyable just as they are.

After your heart is awakened you may feel like a river of compassion runs through your veins. A heightened experience where your Essence is known to be boundless love may swell up within you.

This higher love is natural and effortless. Compassion for our brothers, our sisters and our planet flows through you. You know that we are united as this one love.

This primal blending of consciousness and compassion clears up misconceptions such as the awakened person no longer lives in duality or that she no longer has a personality. There is nothing wrong with duality or with your personality!

The difference is that now you know for yourself how life works. This is not just a belief. It is an intrinsic knowing. It is a certainty. You still use your fascinating unique human personality. You still look the same.

You learn to bask in the abundance of differences. You relish the experience of being separate yet united. This paradoxical beauty of duality is maya.

Via your direct knowing you experience the striking contradictions of maya as an illusion. What a fantastic illusion it is! This crystal clear recognition unfolds as an organic, natural and spontaneous way of behaving and being in the unconditioned ever new now.

Our first awakening is Self-recognition. Then our enlightenment deepens.

We discover how to lovingly acknowledge the uniqueness of each one we meet and connect with. This accepting of consciousness as the manifestation in each unique individual explodes as compassion in us, for us and as us.

I am you. You are me. Yet I am clearly me and you are definitely you!

We are all each a precious part of this grand amazing Wholeness. Heart and consciousness melt together in gratitude and wordless wonder. This unfolding is forever.

Twin Flame Destiny

I had been completely faithful in my marriage for sixteen years. The thought of being any other way never crossed my mind. I had been wild as a teenager and in my early twenties. I was ready to move on. I had my fun!

I was appalled by infidelity. I judged my friends who were not loyal to their husbands. Too many couples pretend to be happy when in fact they are miserable. I did not want to be that kind of phony unhappy person.

I value honesty, integrity and truth. At 26 years old I met my ex-husband and the father of my three children. I had vowed in my heart then and there to be a faithful, loyal and good wife. I wanted to be a mother above all else.

It came to me intuitively that I would have all my kids by the age of 30. This was a deep instinctive intuitive knowing. I was totally certain about it.

At 28 years old I found out I was pregnant with triplets. We were beyond excited. This was the happiest and most thrilling experience of my life up to that point. My body became the vessel for three beautiful human beings. I loved being pregnant.

As I write these words in 2019, my children are now teenagers. Being triplets, they all have the same birthday. They are now 17 years old!

The years after my beautiful perfect babies were born were incredibly busy. They were tremendously rewarding years. I loved being a mother. It brought me tremendous fulfillment. My children mean the world to me. They are my heart. My love for them is boundless.

I was determined to be a good wife and an excellent hands-on mom. I never wanted housekeepers to raise my children. I never wanted to ever get divorced. I wanted my marriage to work. I really did try everything.

I knew that statistically marriage is hard with just one baby. But with three babies at once it was much harder than we had ever imagined. We did both try to make it work. The nonstop busyness, lack of sleep and having to take care of three children at once all by myself took its toll on my marriage.

In what felt like a blink of an eye, my children were active independent teenagers! Suddenly I was needed much less. I had ignored my emotional suffering for many years.

I had been suffering for many years from immeasurable loneliness. After the triplets were born intimacy of any kind was rare in our marriage. Like two ships lost at sea, powerful invisible tides ripped us apart. We drifted further and further away until we were living totally separate lives. We talked about practical matters having to do with our kids. That was it.

Whatever connection we had had in the beginning died. Perhaps you have been in a loveless lifeless marriage or relationship? It is a special kind of hell!

You're both so busy maintaining appearances. The apple is shiny on the outside. You keep polishing it. But inside it is rotten to the core. You live on the surface and pretend that everything is okay.

Ironically, I ended up staying in a phony unhappy marriage like the friends I used to criticize. Also like them I had an affair! This is just one example of how I saw my past judgments literally materialize in front of me to haunt me and taunt me. Karma can be a real bitch — and an incredible teacher!

My mom radar had picked my ex-husband because he was a strong healthy acclaimed star athlete. He had good genes written all over him! I made a great choice in that sense. My teenagers are tall, healthy, strong and smart.

It turned out that we had nothing in common except our kids. We were not interested in the same things. Our communication became non-existent.

This was the hardest part for me. I feel I really tried. I did not want to give up. I had made a commitment to our marriage and I wanted to honor it. I knew something was very wrong. I knew this because I was unhappy and desperately lonely all the time.

I was raised to pretend that everything is okay even when it isn't. I was taught to put a phony smile on my face and pretend to be happy. If I wasn't acting like I was happy I was sent to my room and told to not come out until I was happy! My real feelings were not acceptable to my parents.

I was used to acting as if I was fine and life was wonderful even if it was a living hell. I did not want to admit to myself or to my parents that my marriage had failed. I was faking it to make it. But it was destined to break apart anyway.

I prayed at night often. Late at night I cried for hours on my bathroom floor. What was I praying for? What did I want? Why exactly was I crying?

I wanted to meet someone who would understand me. I was not looking for a lover. I was looking for a friend. I wanted to meet "my person." I wanted to meet someone who was genuinely living the truth that I had discovered.

My loneliness was debilitating. I felt like a hollow robot. My days were busy doing mom errands like buying groceries and clothes and shoes for my kids. I would go for a run every day with three other moms. I cooked and cleaned. Keeping our big house clean kept me busy when I ran out of other things to do.

I spent as much time as possible with my kids. My afternoons were filled with schlepping the three of them back and forth to their various activities. It helped that my ex-husband was a hands-on dad who shared the driving and watched their sporting events.

I was an ardent seeker. Every spare moment alone was spent reading and studying. I was consumed by my studies of the various religions and mysticism. I then progressed to the occult and finally to non-duality.

Then, completely out of the blue, I had not one but two deep awakenings!

These awakenings — the first of Unity on a cold winter day in early 2014 and the second of Infinite Love on a gorgeous summer day later that year — changed everything!

Unfortunately, my radical awakening did not come with instructions.

I did not know what to do with my new intuitive knowing of truth. I had no idea how to rework my life into an integrated vehicle for sharing the unbounded Self I had realized. I knew I was an individual yet now I lived as one with all in my new non-separated way of being.

I laughed at my new dilemma. How simple, easy and naïve being unhappy and lonely seemed to me now. I had been protected from the truth by my ignorance. That would no longer be possible. For me now truth was all that mattered. My world would be shattered beyond recognition.

I Meet My Twin Flame

Please understand that I did not have a clue about such a thing as a Twin Flame. Although I had for decades studied religion, mysticism, occultism and non-duality, I considered psychic abilities, soul mates, UFOs and other new age concepts "woo-woo." In other words, they were total nonsense!

It was now February 2016. My awakenings had taken place two years ago in 2014. In 2015 it had dawned on me that I could look for somebody who would listen to me and talk with me heart to heart. I knew I was not the only person who had awakened. There were others like me.

My guru hunt was not for a teacher. I was already awakened. I was looking for a spiritual friend. My brother had connections that enabled me to meet face to face with some of the most famous spiritual teachers.

I insisted on a personal encounter. No way was I going to sit in the back of the room and hope for something to happen. I'm an Enneagram Eight! I'm going to make it happen! I got my one on one meetings!

I just want you to know that I started at the top. For example, I had coffee with Deepak Chopra. I left no stone unturned. I met some of the most amazing teachers on the planet.

There was nothing wrong with these teachers or the others I met on spiritual retreats. But I knew they were not *the one*.

I have read hundreds and hundreds spiritual books over the years. There was one that had really spoken to me. It is called *The Spiritual Heart*. It was by a spiritual teacher named Ramaji. I had read it several years back.

According to his book, he lived in the San Diego area not far from me. I went to his website and ordered a session. He emailed me and explained that he had just moved to a mountain community east of San Diego. Sessions were online sessions. I demanded a face to face meeting.

"There's boxes everywhere," he protested. I had paid the maximum for my session on purpose. You want money? Then I will give it to you. I refused to back down. He realized that opposing me was futile. We set a date via email.

February 16, 2016. It was a Tuesday. I had arranged for my kids to be picked up from school. He lived 45 minutes away. I felt very excited as I drove to his home in the mountains. This was nothing new. Every time I was about to meet a new teacher I felt this excitement and anticipation.

I arrived early. It was around noon when I knocked on his front door.

The second he opened the door I was hit with an unmistakable knowing. I instantly felt I was meeting the other half of myself. I felt immediately that this stranger I had never met was as much a part of me as I am.

I did not know it then, but this 65 year-old married guru Ramaji was my Twin Flame and life partner. This meeting was the most bizarre and unexpected event of my entire life. I experienced a magical knowing the moment I met him. In that moment I knew that he was me and that I was him. We were one soul!

I felt everything about him. I knew his life and his being just as I know my own Self. An irresistible force of enormous magnitude took me over. I was not just swept away. I was absolutely taken over by an impossibly overwhelming force. All control was gone.

From the moment he opened his door our fate was sealed. Our Twin Flame destiny took over. Our life paths fused together permanently. We who had been one when we began our human journey would now be one again!

I had not forgotten that I was married. I knew that and I knew that I had three kids I loved with all my heart. That first meeting was very professional. We did take a walk in the woods near his place after our session was over. Oddly, we were both wearing black top and bottom.

We found a bench overlooking a beautiful setting with big boulders, tall leafy trees and a rambling dry creek bed. Out of the blue, he started talking about Twin Flames. He had had a session with two people just weeks ago who claimed to be Twin Flames.

He then offered to look at our past lives together. I thought "Okay, he's coming onto me now! It's the old 'we were incredible hot lovers in a past life' line." After all, I was a pretty girl in my 40s. He was in his 60s.

Instead, something strange and unexpected happened. He closed his eyes and did what he does to see past lives. "This is crazy," he said. "I've had five major spiritual lifetimes. You are in every single one of them!"

I could tell he was shaken by this revelation. "I have met people who were in one of my pivotal spiritual lives. But nobody has been in all five of my enlightened lifetimes." His eyes narrowed as he looked at me. "Nobody except you."

He mentioned one of our lives together. He saw it like a movie. He was a Buddhist monk. I was a Buddhist nun. We were in Thailand. We were in love.

The only contact we had was over a wall that divided the monastery from the nunnery. Our eyes would meet in noble silence. We never spoke.

Wordlessly we would encourage each other with our eyes to reach nirvana and achieve enlightenment. This we knew was the highest love.

Ramaji would not say more. Later I learned that this theme of separation or of being together yet not being able to be truly and totally together as man and woman was a common Twin Flame theme. Only in their final lifetime are they able to unite fully and completely in every way. Even then it is not all just romance. They are united in a mission to help humanity in a big way.

My fears that he would be a dog were groundless. The anticipated moves never materialized. He did not make any kind of gesture to hug me or kiss me. He did not try to hold my hand when we walked back to his home.

He was the perfect gentleman. Not only did he keep his distance, I could tell that he was keeping his energy towards me neutral. He was so neutral that it bothered me. Okay, you're not going to hit on me. But give me something!

I knew I was married with three teenagers. I knew he was married. I did not believe that what I was feeling was humanly possible. I did not understand what was happening. I had never felt anything like this in my life.

On the outside everything looked polite and professional. On the inside, I was a changed woman. I was in love. This was the love at first sight I had heard about but never experienced.

I easily sensed everything about him and his life. He was me. He was my other half. I knew who he was. I knew things I should not have known.

All of it was automatic and effortless. An enormous undeniable power was pulling us together like a super magnet. Like a giant hand, destiny had picked us up from our separate lives and put us down again on a new life path where we would be together. The inevitable had already happened.

A romantic Twin Flame union is unique and unusual in many ways. It is impossible to describe with words. It is an unlimited love in the form of a fiery romance as pure and innocent as it is passionate and real.

The trance psychic Edgar Cayce talked about Twin Flames. He called them twin souls. In the beginning, he said, "male and female were as one."

Our Emotional Affair Gets Physical

I walked up the hill. There were lots of big green trees on my left and the road, the main drag in this small mountain town, was on my right. I had arrived at the destination my TF and I had agreed to a few days beforehand.

I had kept asking for another physical meeting. He said he was happy with our emails and our online emotional affair. He wanted to keep a safe distance away from me!

He did not trust himself around me. Like me, he had strong convictions about marriage. He didn't believe in having an affair either.

He had finally agreed to see me in person. I had no idea why I was there. There was nothing logical about what I was doing. I had a deep knowing that there was nowhere else I could be. I had surrendered to this knowing.

My rational mind was incapable of any argument. My conscience was completely aware of what was going on. This meeting simply had to happen.

This was our second physical meeting. As soon as I saw him I was again struck by the love, compassion and intuitive knowing I had felt beforehand around him. He grabbed my hand without a single word.

We walked toward my car. It felt as if I was reborn to be right here! It felt as if no time had passed in which we had functioned as two different people.

The merging was instant. It was wordless and it was truth! Subsequently I have read a few books on Twin Flame unions. They do not do it justice. I cannot express these feelings in words. Neither could those authors.

We drove for a few minutes and found a side street with a patch of grass. We sat on a blanket under a tree. We hugged and kissed. We kissed only a few times. It was amazing. We melted into each other like streams of hot butter. Just hugging him felt heavenly. Our innocent hug and kiss transcended every other man-woman encounter I had known.

Just holding him in my arms was more thrilling and fulfilling that any kind of sex I had ever had! For both of us, this first day of physical contact remains precious and unforgettable. We were astonished at the beauty and intensity of our feelings for each other.

At this point, we had no idea about our future. We both felt taken over by this magnetic pull. We did not resist what was happening. We both chose to surrender to it. We could not resist it and we knew we should not resist it.

Our bodies were two halves of a magnet. These magnetic halves had but one option. To move towards each other and unite as one whole soul.

A true Twin Flame union is extremely rare. A big age gap is common. Or there are other significant differences to deal with. It is not a walk in the park. There are many challenging situations that must be overcome.

We both felt our souls had agreed to unite at this time to help the world. Our high intoxicating love vibration infused our shared life mission. It did not take us long to figure this out. Even though I felt skeptical, my skepticism was drowned by the force of my pure knowing and this miraculous love.

Though I was madly in love, our emotional online affair shocked and horrified me. I desperately wanted to go back in time and reverse this force but I could not stop it. I had no idea what was happening to me. I knew instinctively that I was abandoning my moral compass.

Everything that I thought I stood for as a human being was being challenged. Still I could only think about him. I could only be with him. I knew from the moment we met that this man was what I had been looking for all my life. I knew he was my person. I knew that he was my home.

One thing led to another and I did what I swore I would never do. I saw where it was going but I could do nothing about it. I was helpless.

Our relationship had been friendly and extremely close but platonic in every way. It was strictly professional in the beginning.

I am an artist. We talked about how I could illustrate a book he was working on or use one of my painting as the book cover. However, in a few short months I realized that I had fallen head over heels in love with him.

I recognized our daily emails were now what is called an "emotional affair." I could feel how the years of being misunderstood, the years of being shut down with no communication, the years of no feeling, the years of fear, were suddenly being dissolved and released via this person I now called my Twin Flame.

Even before we physically consummated our love I felt tremendous shame and guilt. I could not sleep or eat. Yet I could not stop myself. it was beyond my control. I had merged with him. I was not able to do anything about it.

Our melted hearts had become one! He was the very person I had been praying for. I just never imagined I could find a best friend and lover too.

The lover part of our online romance happened several months later in late May. Two weeks after that meeting I asked my ex-husband for a divorce.

We were both completely immersed in doing our best not to hurt or harm anyone. It was an unexpected and major event in my life. It was the biggest life change ever in my outer reality.

I somehow knew what needed to be done. It was crazy, bizarre and spontaneous. I did it knowing there would be consequences although I had no clue just how shocking and massive these consequences would be. A huge part of me simply felt I had no choice.

A natural and effortless love flows between us like a river. We finish each other's thoughts. We understand the voiceless messages of the heart and feel our togetherness at every moment. Even when we are not physically together I always feel him right with me. Always. He is my heart. My soul is complete. It was completed the moment we met.

The Domino Effect

The domino effect that took over when my family discovered my affair is a story all its own. After I was exposed for lying to my ex-husband, my children and my parents about the fact that our affair began while we were both still married, my life began to tumble down like a house of cards.

My conscious motivation had been to protect my teenagers. However, the universe did not allow for any falseness on my part. I was caught by my kids – the very ones I was trying to protect! They got hold of my private emails to Ramaji and distributed them to my ex-husband and to my parents.

I remembered that my Kabbalah teacher had often said that the road to evil is often led by the best intentions. Her words echoed in my mind.

The next few years were devastating and humiliating beyond words. I desperately tried everything I could to redeem myself in their naive and innocent eyes. As a parent this was the most traumatic and hideous experience imaginable.

The fact that my life partner was also getting divorced because of me only added to my pain. I felt enormous shame and guilt regarding his ex-wife!

This karmic blowback was lived in real time. I took the knocks and paid for it in full. I lay in bed praying for forgiveness. I beat myself up for months.

I was face to face with the natural law of cause and effect. The effect was as clear as can be and the cause had been our affair! I came to understand that in our times the distance in time and space between cause and effect is much shorter. For me it was instantaneous!

Eventually whatever we cause will have an effect for good or bad. Today we are seeing accelerated in real time what our individual and collective causes have produced in our world. As a collective we must own our collective fear-based agreements. Then we can create fresh agreements made in love.

In my case I had raised my kids in a false way from the start! I had been afraid of living my truth. Had I been totally honest about my marriage in the beginning, I would have gotten divorced when they were babies.

The extreme fallout from my divorce was the result of this fear-based agreement. It had all come full circle. I was able to feel my pain, acknowledge my mistake and make a new love-based agreement anchored in my truth. In order for me to live in a totally honest present that was filled with real love, I had to take complete responsibility for my past.

Armed with the new dirt on me and my affair, my ex-husband had a field day. He confirmed the cruel and demeaning opinion of me that I had suffered for more than a decade. My pain and suffering from his verbal attacks made me physically shake.

I apologized to my children day in and day out. I welcomed their hurt and anger. I understood their need to blame and condemn me. I let their process unfold naturally.

They were able to forgive me. It took two years. After they had discharged their disappointment from my betrayal their big pure hearts found space for forgiving me.

During this time frame my parents and brother stopped talking to me. I had decided to not go to my brother's wedding overseas. I had not been able to emotionally connect with his new wife at all. It was the worst timing imaginable in my life. My children and I were really suffering. It was just all too much!

My parents, my brother and his fiancé were fully aware of all the difficulties I was having with my ex-husband and my kids. Yet they expected me to slap on a big smile and dance a happy dance about my brother getting married! They offered me no sympathy, no emotional support and no understanding.

Even after my children had forgiven me, I was still working on forgiving myself. Not for my decision to get divorced or to love my Twin Flame. I knew we had to be together. I could not forgive myself for hurting my children in any way, shape or form.

Our divorces subjected us to severe judgments from people we thought were friends. This was a consequence that we had to face. But no judgment by anyone else was able to match how I was judging myself.

I began to see the fear and toxic shame that I had lived with all my life in a new light. I was deeply dreading my family's judgment. I knew what was in store for us. I knew that our relationship would seem bizarre to them.

I had decided to hide our affair for as long as possible. I was afraid they would not accept my choices. They would not understand how I could cheat on my ex-husband. They would not understand my choice to love an older man who is a spiritual teacher.

As the house of cards I called my life collapsed into a pile of rubble around my feet, I had to face truths I had always known yet refused to see. My own parents and my own brother did not know me. They did not understand me. The brutal truth was that they didn't want to know me or understand me!

The family I had loved and admired did not reach out, call or visit during the hardest time of my life. This was after being a devoted loyal daughter and sister for 45 years.

When my words, behaviors and emotional need for them to listen to me exceeded their tolerance levels, they took steps to erase me from their lives. It was as if I had never existed. I was cast out into an ice-cold wilderness like a stranger. Their stony silence and total indifference broke my heart

My fears, my lies and negative beliefs physically manifested in front of me in dramatic fashion. I was caught red-handed, punished, humiliated and cast aside by my entire family. This was the hardest, most disturbing and most confusing time of my entire life. I suffered immeasurable guilt and shame.

I tolerated an onslaught of incredibly cruel insults and slurs from my ex. This became a constant every day for years before and after he learned that I had had my affair while I was still married to him. My parent's unwillingness to talk about my life partner with me and their complete dismissal of him as a human being were other warning signs I could no longer ignore.

My life partner patiently nurtured me and loved me through this tough traumatic phase. He knew that I was being emotionally abused. He would listen and cry with me as each penny dropped. He patiently allowed me the space to feel and express every feeling.

He listened as I let go of my need to be blindly loyal and to project my perfect image onto my parents and brother. He listened as I finally allowed myself to feel decades of unacknowledged built-up emotions. I did not believe this much heartache and suffering was possible.

Each feeling surfaced in an extreme and overwhelming way. The process was uncontrollable. All I had the strength for were my tears. I did not think the crying would ever stop. I did not believe that I would survive the dark realizations that were flooding into me from my unconsciousness.

Rivers of emotion would rush through my body all day every day. I allowed it all. I knew I could not stop it. I knew I should not stop it. My awakening had taught me that resistance is futile. I prayed for mercy. I begged on hands and knees for the pain to end.

My life had changed beyond recognition. The family that I had felt closest to, my parents and my brother, had become cold-hearted strangers.

Words cannot describe my disappointment in my family. Their indifferent silence was as astonishing to me as it was devastating. I felt I had lost it all!

Owning and letting go of my projections (projecting my goodness on them) and my introjections (taking in their darkness as mine) was the final stage. This stage of seeing how I create my experience via my interpretation of it then smoothly transitioned into pure seeing and the deep integration of my awakening into my new radically transformed life.

This transformation had come over me like the tidal wave in my prophetic dream. That dramatic dream was now my reality. In my dream I knew I could not die. In this reality I wished I could!

My false idealizations down to the very last drop were swept away by the massive power of this mountainous tidal wave. My awakening was not the end. It was the beginning.

In the morning when you wake up you don't just lay in bed all day. You wake up, get dressed and start living. Waking up is forgotten!

Our Twin Flame Spiritual Mission

The moment of meeting my Twin Flame was surreal and astonishing. For the very first time in my life I felt totally seen and heard! As soon as I was with my Twin Flame, the man who would become my lover, my business partner and my life partner, I felt I had arrived home.

My future partner was mesmerized by me at our first meeting. He openly respected my two decades of spiritual study. He instantly acknowledged that I had already had such a deep awakening that I could not be his student.

He told me that I was already at LOC 1000! I was already a Self-realized person. He knew that I knew. He said it was obvious to him.

This unexpected validation swept through me like a welcome torrent of rain on a thirsty bone-dry desert. It was the first time anyone had ever wholeheartedly affirmed me and my worth. I felt deeply valued and authenticated. I felt like I mattered. It was big for me.

It wasn't just what he said. It was how he looked at me. He looked at me like I was his equal!

Half an hour into our session he said "What do you want to do?" He smiled sheepishly. He was out of ideas! That's when I suggested that we take our walk on the beautiful forested property that he lived on at the time.

Something magnificent and unmistakable happened at that first meeting. He felt it too. He confessed later that he didn't know what to make of me. He became fascinated by me. He couldn't get me out of his head.

I fell in love with him on that first day. It took him a few months. He told me later that he had wanted to make sure this was what I really wanted. He took it slow in order to protect me. He knew that my divorce would bring about massive changes in my life.

I wish I could describe the incredibly romantic, special, strange and exquisite bond we share with better words. But I can't. There simply are no words!

Our business partnership had an enormous positive impact on me. My partner trusted me completely. He believed in me. He was this way in both our romantic relationship and our business relationship.

This felt wonderfully good to me. No person had ever seen me or listened to me or believed in me like this. We felt instant trust. We want only happiness for each other. It is more than love. We adore each other.

I know that our bond is unbreakable because we both want the same thing. We both want to serve mankind and help people awaken. It is a burning passion that we share. The universe brought us together for this purpose.

His love saved my life. It is not just that we have gotten along like a house on fire from day one.

He has told me many times that I am the only person he has ever met where every conversation we have is at the highest level. He never has to compromise or hold back or water down what he is saying. It is a source of unlimited joy for both of us to be able to talk as two people who have awakened to the true Self. This alone would justify our relationship!

He began training me to be a spiritual teacher in the second half of 2016. We began leading groups together in January 2017. I started doing one on one sessions with my own students soon after.

I was so excited to see the quick progress the students made. I felt relieved that I was earning some money so soon. It helped relieve my financial stress as a single mom with three teenagers. I was able to give my father back the money he had been giving me to help my family after my divorce.

Deep down I was still the little girl hoping to be seen with love and feelings of respect and pride. This was something my parents would proudly admit they did not do. "We do not see our children through rose colored glasses!"

I heard this critical sentence so many times it became my childhood mantra. Internally I translated their words into a message of "I am terribly flawed. I am not good enough. My parents do not love me just as I am!"

At 43 years old I was still trying to get the attention and recognition I had longed for from my parents. But as a mom I could only see my children's perfection. I was not like my parents. I loved my children unconditionally.

My parents cannot tolerate being challenged. As an Enneagram Eight, my very nature is to be the Challenger! I never felt I could just be myself.

I was always walking on eggshells. I was constantly worried that I would say or do something wrong. Their way of dealing with me was to criticize me. One look would scare me into silence. I was afraid of my own parents.

Another favorite saying of theirs that my mother repeated to me often was "Children are to be seen, not heard!" In other words… SHUT UP! I was left starving for the acceptance, recognition and validation that never came.

In sharp contrast, it is my life partner's joy to shower me with love, acceptance, recognition and validation. We effortlessly give each other the precious gifts of our undivided attention, devotion and adoration. We delight in saying and doing that which will increase each other's happiness.

I too had learned to listen. I too had learned to love. At long last my love was felt and appreciated. I felt this appreciation for the first time ever. My partner was loving me in a way I had never known before. I felt deeply nurtured. I felt I mattered as a human being. I felt profoundly respected.

This love gave me the confidence to see myself as an independent thinker with something valuable to say. I was no longer mind controlled. I was no longer intimidated or scared. I could now see how my conditioning had kept me in a golden prison. The key to escape my jail cell was in my hand.

Love is my key. Now I can fuse my "Pink World" — my private world of perfect total love — with the so-called "real" world "out there." Love has become my world.

Love had indeed conquered all... but it had taken a war!

Insight

Desire

"The easiest way to get what you want is to help others get what they want."

— Deepak Chopra

During my Kabbalah years I received valuable teachings that helped me understand the nature of desire. Desire to BE is the key to life itself.

In non-dual circles you may hear that desire is a bad thing. Desire is shakti. It is our beloved life force. Never attempt to crush your life force!

When you study the nature of desire itself and how it works universally you will create the needed consciousness around it. My Kabbalah teacher called this consciousness "The desire to receive for the sake of sharing."

The unconscious alternative is "Receiving for the sake of self alone." This is how desire got its bad reputation. Receiving for self alone makes people robotic takers. They cannot see that sharing is the way of the universe.

Look around you. How does this universe really work?

Can you see how everything is always sharing itself with everything else? Our universe is a system that is driven by sharing and receiving.

A good example of this is rainfall. The water vapor rises and creates clouds. The clouds become plump and full of moisture. They get more and more full and plump until they cannot contain themselves any longer.

At their moment of total fullness they burst open. Rain cascades over the earth, over the pastures, the farms, the forests and the jungles. This beautiful rain is the moisture needed by the leafy green trees and the exquisite flowers for their growth. The fields can now produce the vegetables we need for our desired food.

We nourish ourselves in order to have energy and an abundance of life force. Thanks to the rain we can be healthy and survive. Then we in turn make our unique individual contributions to life.

This is the natural flow of events. The entire universe works in these ways that are magical and miraculous.

When you become conscious of your desires as part of this flow and see that you and all human beings are a part of the whole, you will create conscious awareness around your desires. You will see that creation as you, me and all of us is desiring whatever it desires with the intention to share its anticipated abundance with others. You are now working consciously in union with creation as it is.

When you can see the intrinsic value in sharing, this is followed by a recognition of the intrinsic value in receiving. The receiving is just as important as the sharing. When you receive consciously you *are* sharing!

When you can consciously receive with joy, anticipation and appreciation you are receiving with love for the sharer or the giver. The process can now complete itself because you are conscious and aware of this cycle. You are now desiring to receive for the sake of sharing.

Just imagine winning a huge jackpot. If you won 10 million dollars what is the first thing that you would do? You would call your family and friends to SHARE this great news!

The expansive joyful fullness of this fantastic win and the reality of receiving millions of dollars will be automatically followed by the natural need to explode and share the news of this amazing event!

This is natural law. It is in operation all the time. It is critical that we raise our awareness around sharing and receiving. This is the path to bliss, joy and abundance. In order to experience these fully in your life learn to share and to receive with this consciousness.

As a teacher I'm always sharing my Self or whatever I know with my students. Their gift to me is receiving my knowledge.

Their receiving gives me the bliss that no self-oriented state can give. This outcome is inevitable because I'm consciously acting in accordance with natural law. I do my work with this awareness always.

Receiving for the sake of sharing is the secret golden key to making your desires a blessing for you and for everybody in your life. Receiving for the sake of sharing puts you in harmony with your environment and makes you a part of the solution whatever you do and wherever you go.

Receiving for the sake of sharing is the proven formula for a wonderful life!

The Akashic Records

Soon after my first awakening that occurred during meditation, I decided to meet with a woman who combined breathing techniques and dancing. A girlfriend who is a mom from my children's school had recommended her.

I was going through a lot of confusion. I was happy to meet with any like-minded person in case they could shed light on my new consciousness.

My experience with her was fun. My curiosity was satisfied. I thought that was it. As I was leaving, I had to walk down a narrow flight of steps. On the way down this flight of steps I encountered a man coming up.

He looked like maybe he was Hispanic. He did not look like he was from around here. He was friendly and said hi to me. It turned out that the lady I had just seen was waiting for him.

She introduced us. I found myself asking him questions. There was something about him that intrigued me. He had a unique energy.

He was visiting from Peru. He told me he was a reader of the Akashic Records. His years in Peru were spent with a shaman who taught him many things including how to do this kind of reading.

He asked me if I had time for a reading. I did. I was not at all familiar with the Akashic Records. His unusual vibration made me interested in what he had to offer. That is the only reason. I do not typically get "readings"!

We sat down opposite one another. He asked me for my permission to look at my personal Akashic Records. I agreed. We closed our eyes for about two minutes. Then he told me to open my eyes.

He was staring at me. "You are a very big soul!" he said. He was stumbling for words. "Your consciousness at birth... It was like you said to yourself... Not again!" He looked at me intensely. "You did the master a huge favor!"

He continued. "Perhaps there is something you need to say. Forget all the books you are reading. It can be said in your own way!"

I felt deeply confused by his message. I had no clue what he was talking about. Soon we closed our eyes again. Our brief session was over.

I pondered his "Not again!" statement. I remembered my mother telling me that she almost had a miscarriage while pregnant with me. She started to bleed. The doctor wanted to remove me, her pregnancy, immediately.

I was to be her firstborn child. My mother was extremely upset. She did not want to abort her baby. My father asked the doctor if they could wait until the morning. By morning her bleeding had stopped. I was born seven months later. I think she was three months pregnant when this occurred.

A reluctance about being born made sense but the rest was quite strange for me. It is only now, five years later, that I fully comprehend what that unusual man told me.

The master I came to help is Ramaji, my Twin Flame life partner. This book *Intimacy with the Infinite* is the "something I need to say in my own way" that the Peruvian shaman predicted back in the spring of 2014!

Insight

You Can't Become What You Already Are

"Knowing others is wisdom. Knowing yourself is enlightenment."

— Lao Tzu

Many people long to be enlightened. I was one of them. It is something that our seeking ego wants so badly. Only an ego can want to wake up. Our Essence or true Self knows it is always wide awake right here right now!

What we learn through this bizarre awakening and post-awakening journey is that enlightenment is the seeing through of that very ego which desired the glorious self-aggrandizement that it imagined awakening to be.

Enlightenment is the decimation, destruction and irreversible understanding of the conceited little one who thought it was not awake! It is the wholesale annihilation of the little me that wanted to awaken in the first place.

This is not an extinction. It is a rebirth and a regeneration. Just please understand that the one who returns from this heroic journey into the unknown may look and sound like the old person, but she is not!

She is now a three-dimensional hologram being perfectly projected by divine consciousness. This was always the case but now she consciously knows it.

We do not lose our personality. We can still operate as we always have. It has nothing to do with not having an ego, small me, small I or small self.

In order to live as sane functional human beings, we need her too! In her own unforgettably funky fantastic way, she is perfect too!

It is the *knowing* that shifts. There is now the intuitive certainty and unshakable existential knowing that although my little I continues to operate in my daily life she is my servant just as I am now the big Self.

She is not my master. I am the master. I use her when I need her. She goes back to her place when I do not need her. Truth runs this show now!

Now unfolds the new and unforeseeable endless journey. We are discovering how to be totally authentic and how to embody truth. We are claiming it as who and what we really are under all circumstances.

We are now being and living in a fresh new way. This arrives at the cost of all that was old. The little me from the past no longer gets joy from being who she is not. Authenticity is the only currency of value.

All of this takes time. Integration takes time. It does not happen overnight.

Even so, what you have lost looms large. What have you gained?

You have gained the freedom to be precisely as you really are. This is your "true I" that you have always been and will always be. To live this way is a lot harder than most people, even teachers, are willing to admit.

We have all been deeply conditioned. We have been molded and shaped from the second we are born. We were literally taught who we should be, how we should act and what we should think. We have been programmed to believe that there is something terribly wrong with us.

This puts us on a sterile treadmill of thankless self-improvement. Since we are flawed and bad, we cannot allow ourselves to just BE.

God forbid we should be happy now just as we are! The Big Lie is that we must become something that we are not if we ever hope to grab that gossamer dream called happiness!

Rarely are we encouraged to just be ourselves. After our parents install our early programming that we are just this "little me," we get subjected to a rigid educational system. It trains us as tiny children to blindly submit to authority and memorize and repeat outright lies like helpless parrots.

Thinking for yourself is frowned upon if not forbidden. When you challenge the status quo and ask provocative questions you get punished.

Awakening is a miracle. It is remarkable that it happens at all. Our massive conditioning from birth succeeds at enslaving the majority. But there are some, often in childhood, who sense the falseness and intuit the truth.

In awakening we realize who we really are. Strangely we already were that person. We are a perfect pure being and we were always perfect and pure.

The weird cynical belief pattern that as human beings we are just a selfish toxic mess is only an agreement that we made for the sake of our survival. It drives us to fight, compete and even kill for rocks when diamonds fill our pockets. We yearn to find a bigger box when in fact we are freer than birds.

In the ultimate irony we fight to the death for our own limitations! We were not taught to love and honor our own beautiful Self. We were not taught to love and accept others just as they are. Yet to do so is our very nature.

The little ego me wants to be someone she is not. This is the problem and it is the solution. Propelled by this mirage of being able to acquire a golden future, we have the possibility of exhausting our little selves to such a grand extent that we simply cannot keep up the exhausting pretense.

We inadvertently stumble over the cliff of no return and surrender the search in a single timeless unplanned moment. We see through our perceived limitations and imperfections. We know that they are but the costume of the day. We see that in fact the emperor has no clothes!

To feel lost and confused when seeking truth is normal and even desirable. You should be asking "What is true?" when clearly you do not yet know.

Before the arrival of truth it is common for the seeker to dwell in a dark difficult state of overwhelming doubt. It is this special spiritual doubt that splits open the wall of illusion and dissolves the old, the small and the false.

We must challenge and question the appearance until we see huge cracks in its distorting magic. We fight for mindful insight instead of for mindless entertainment. The matrix is real. Just turn on your phone or television.

It is here in this confusing crisis, in the doubt, in the abyss, in the black hole, in the dark night, that the real true magician awaits. She is here always. She is waiting patiently for *you* to recognize the real You and see with revolutionary clarity Who and What you really are!

This gigantic knowing goes far beyond mere recognition. It transcends any and all limiting belief patterns. All your life you were in a secret identity crisis. Now at long last you know who you really are. Now at long last you are being your true Self. The relief you feel is staggering beyond words.

Now you know your own true Self. You are it now and you were always it now. It cannot be compared to anything else. That is why it is called the absolute. It is the ultimate solvent. Everything dissolves into it.

YOU ARE THAT!

What about the past?

The past can be left there just where it is. You will access it as needed. Go on and you can know yourself as an ever-new person second by second.

As this undeniable shift takes over, you allow all your old stuff to filter through you. All that is false dissolves in this natural effortless process.

You become more and more confident and sure of your new true Self. You begin to embody and own your truth. It is not an egocentric shallow or immature confidence. It is not a heightened state that comes and goes.

It is a rock-solid diamond-like awareness that you know to be the unmistakably authentic stateless state. The state you are in right now, whatever that state may be, is that stateless state! The state you are in right now as you read this is the perfect unstained stateless state!

The freedom to be and to fully feel whatever comes up takes over. The more you allow yourself this freedom and express it, the more freedom you begin to embody and the more boundlessly you enjoy your life exactly as it is. Though there are obvious limitations to the analogy, to say that you become like a happy carefree little child again is not far from the truth!

You are both the magician and the magic. When you discover your imperial ruling status it is a major release. No longer will you depend on anyone or anything outside of your true Self.

All the power is in your hands. This Unity that has never known division is everything. Anything you might want is already yours for You Are That!

Nothing is left out. How can there be anything that is not that too?

This infinite abundance is your inheritance! It is your birthright to be who you are and claim your fabulous vast fortune!

You will laugh until you cry. You will dance and sing. You will get on your knees and thank the Source of all of this with tears flowing like rivers.

You will discover the supermassive love that moves the world without moving.

There is nothing more precious than the ability to feel. Your capacity to feel your precious human feelings will now include and overtake your whole body. There will be no more blocks to the expansion of your aliveness.

You will bask in the glory of being without definitions or conditioning.

Spontaneous reverence and wonder will overwhelm you now that you can finally feel, express and be the big Self you really are without limits.

You will ask yourself "How could I have missed this?"

Then you will laugh at your own question!

Fuck One Goat

Have you heard the expression "Fuck one goat…"?

It was a family joke. When my brother and I were children we would get lectured about the importance of reputation. The joke was that you could have done everything right. You could have built a stellar reputation over many years. But make one big mistake – fuck just one goat – and your reputation is ruined!

I spent 16 years in a silent loveless marriage. I had pretended to be happy. It was a lie. I was not happy at all. This turned out to be a big mistake.

I did this so that my kids could grow up and not go through the trauma of divorce and a broken family. I wanted to have the perfect happy family. But my perfect family was just an image in my head. It was an illusion!

The real result of my choice to live a lie was that my children learned how to *not* have a good relationship. They witnessed two people who could not communicate with each other. The graphic example of a mother who was ignored and shut down got burned into their memories.

My ex-husband and I wanted to be good parents. We both adored our triplets. Our marriage suffered because I was raised to believe that I was always the problem. I was raised to always agree and be subservient.

He had been raised in a toxic family environment too. We did not argue during our marriage. Though we lived together in the same house with our three children, our relationship was cold and lifeless. We literally lived separate lives under the same roof.

My awakening in 2014 rocked my phony world to the core. I was no longer capable of hiding my loneliness from myself. I saw that I was deceiving myself. I deserved to be loved and treated with respect and human dignity!

My kids knew a mother who was a fake! My intention was to protect them. Early in my marriage I decided stay married as long as I could for their sake.

I dedicated myself to being a model mother. I was home except when shopping for food or jogging. I studied spiritual teachings when my kids were at school. I did all my motherly chores happily.

I drove my kids wherever they wanted whenever they wanted. My ex-husband had been a professional athlete. He played golf three times a week.

I cooked and I cleaned constantly. I never drank alcohol. It didn't want our kids to see me drinking. I was a full-time totally committed loving mother! My children were my life! All I ever wanted was to raise my children well. Above all else I wanted them to be happy.

I was a model daughter. I adored and respected my parents. Yet I felt inadequate. I was deeply afraid of them. At the time I was visiting my parents three times a week. I always felt fear when I was around them.

It finally dawned on me that I had been raised to be afraid of them. They subscribed to patriarchal dictator beliefs. Children should be seen and not heard. Children should be controlled. Children must be dominated. They must fear their parents and obey them. Children do not have a voice.

I was shocked. I realized that I had been shut down. My individuality had not been respected or encouraged. I had been taught that it was not okay for me to be myself. I had been taught that I was bad. I had been taught that I was not good enough and that I would never be good enough.

Another shock came when I realized that my marriage was a replay of how my parents had treated me. It was familiar for me to be suppressed and shut down. I had attracted a husband who would duplicate that condition.

I was not looking for a lover or a new relationship when I met my life partner in February 2016. I was just looking for an authentic awakened person who would listen to me and understand my spiritual awakening.

Our meeting led to an online emotional affair. This secret affair culminated late May 2016 in a perfect day filled with fun, laughter and unforgettable lovemaking in a beautiful forest. Not wanting to live a lie, two weeks later I told my husband that I wanted a divorce. I filed for divorce in June 2016.

It did not matter what good I had done up to the time of my affair and divorce. It did not matter how hard I had tried. It did not matter that I had denied my feelings, gone against my true nature and sacrificed my soul for 43 years to act the role of the perfect obedient devoted daughter.

Even though I had sincerely loved my parents, done the best I could to please them and tried in every possible way to earn their approval, in the end it did not matter at all. In the end I was still the troublemaker, still the black sheep, still the problem, still their deeply empathic pathetic patsy.

Fuck one goat!

When I announced my divorce to my parents, I was shocked by my parent's joy at my getting a divorce. They had known all along that he was not good for me they said. We will back you up they said. We will love you they said.

As soon as I filed for divorce my ex and my father turned it into a venomous legal war. My ex-husband said that he had no money. My parents did not believe him. They hired forensic accountants to find his secret stash of cash. They suspected him of hiding offshore accounts.

My parents were indifferent to the terrible impact that this long bitter divorce was having on my three children. My divorce had become a toxic battle to protect their precious money no matter what the cost to me, my teenagers or their father. That they had attacked him I could understand. That they willingly ignored the devastating consequences of their legal fire fight on my family astonished me. But even bigger shocks were waiting for me.

The irony of all of this was that none of the money was mine. The house was not mine. It was owned by my parents. Yes, it was a mansion but it was not mine at all.

My ex-husband knew that my parents were wealthy. He rightfully felt he deserved something for his years as a faithful loyal husband and responsible caring father. He used every trick in the book to counter my father's legal attacks. He used me and our children as human shields. Like my father, all he cared about was winning and money.

Their uncaring attitudes astounded me. No one realized how it felt for me to be in the middle of a war over money that was not mine. It was a living hell to see people I loved become monsters over money.

My divorce was my problem. Not theirs. I felt terrible guilt.

The scales began to fall from my eyes. I saw that my parents were incapable of reaching out. They were incapable of empathy. I could not express to them the many horrible and sad things that were happening daily at our home.

I was still not allowed to complain. Their coldness was so bizarre. They knew that their grandchildren and I were suffering terribly.

They could not allow themselves to *feel*. I began to realize that was the hidden theme in my upbringing. Feelings were forbidden. That was my clue to understanding my irrational feelings of worthlessness and inadequacy.

I had never been allowed to simply voice my truth. Instead I lived my life protecting everyone around me. This divorce was the first and only time I had needed their emotional support and protection.

Only my life partner and my best female friend would listen. I have them to thank for saving my sanity over this terrible destructive time in my life.

I had one affair in 16 years and left my husband two weeks later. Filing for divorce immediately was the honest thing to do. My life partner and I had begun working together. I told everybody that it was just a professional business relationship. The reality was that we were now lovers.

I meant no harm. But my choice to cover up the truth compounded the problem. I should have come out and told my parents and my kids the real truth about why I was getting divorced.

Why did I fabricate this big lie? I knew that if my parents and my kids found out that the 65 year-old spiritual guru I was now working with was my boyfriend all hell would break loose. Unfortunately, I was right.

Through a strange quirk of fate the truth came out anyway. I realized that I was not going to be able to get away with even one ounce of pretending. My destiny had determined that I would not get away with even a single lie.

I had lied to protect all my family members. I had lied to protect my beloved kids especially. My kids were enraged and devastated. Their harsh criticism and terrible judgment of me was hell on earth. I was demonized by them. I became a monster in their eyes. I did not blame them. I felt I deserved it.

Worst of all was my fear was that I was going to lose my beloved children! This terrified me. I felt that if I lost my children because of this appalling chain of events then my life would not be worth living.

My parents went on pretending nothing was wrong. They were incapable of offering me any kind of emotional support. Instead their response was to leave the country during my awful ordeal to celebrate my brother's wedding.

My mother insulted and attacked my character because I did not like my brother's fiancé. All I did was voice this opinion one time. That was enough.

In our family system I was not allowed to have my own opinions. I was not allowed to disagree with my parents. I had to align myself with their opinions and views no matter what the personal cost to me.

I was not being allowed to express my depression or my trauma to them. They never came to my house to visit with me or my kids. They never showed warmth or sincere caring. My mother was as cruel and cold as ice.

My brother's new wife — my mother's new daughter in law — was now my mother's new angel. Now more than ever, I was the devil. My mother during this painful time kept insulting me and criticizing me. My own mother was humiliating me, torturing me and gaslighting me.

Though unthinkable for me at the time, she was trying to get rid of me! I had become much more trouble to her than I was worth.

She had found a viable reliable substitute for me. It was time for me to be discarded. My brother's wife was the perfect compliant upgrade. She would play my mother's game and mirror back whatever my mother wanted to hear. My mother seized the opportunity. She was my replacement!

I felt completely confused and utterly devastated. The people I had lived my life for, protected and loved the most had just abandoned me. I realized with a shock that in my 43 years my parents had never apologized to me. Not even one time. I now knew they were incapable of being sorry or empathic.

I was cast aside just as my ex-husband had been. It was as if we had both died. Incredibly, my parents began to act as if I didn't exist. They stopped replying to my emails, texts and phone calls. I vented all my hurt over the course of six months.

It is true that after the fiasco of my brother's marriage, I asked for a time out. But I intended this time to be only a break as we collected ourselves and reflected on the difficult past events. It was never my desire to have no contact with them ever again. I still love them and I always will.

To make matters worse, I was stuck in their home. I could not afford to move. I had not worked for 20 years in order to raise my kids. I felt humiliated and was trying desperately to survive on my own financially.

It was a minor miracle that I was now making what most people would consider a good income as a spiritual teacher. Yet it was not enough to cover the needs and expenses of three active teenagers plus the added cost of renting an apartment.

Not only that, they loved their home with its five big bedrooms, high ceilings, deluxe private movie theater and exquisite tropical backyard on half of an acre. During the summer there could be twenty teenagers in the house or outside playing in the pool.

Furthermore, my father was paying a small fortune for their private high school. The last thing I wanted to do at this point was to disrupt their lives even more by making them relocate from my parent's mansion into a tiny apartment that I could barely afford. To then add to their misery by suddenly forcing them to attend public high school, lose all their friends and shatter their chances at attending a good college was inconceivable to me.

Not only would this further shake their broken world at its foundations, I was terrified that taking this route would drive an additional wedge between me and my kids. I could not afford to take that risk. I had already betrayed them once.

It was a good thing perhaps that I was relieved of that decision since I could not afford to make such a move in the first place. I am eternally grateful that my parents allowed us to stay in their home and continued paying for their grandchildren's education.

I was told by my mother during this traumatic time that I was so much worse after meeting my life partner. My family never gave him a chance. I did not understand what "worse" meant? All I had done is love them, visit them and include them. Yet my parents ended up dismissing me like an outcast.

I felt like I was going crazy.

All I had ever wanted was their approval. I yearned to be loved, respected and validated by them. In the past, the one thing I did get a few moments of approval for was being a good wife and mother!

But due to the piling on of one massive stress after another, by late 2018 I was a total wreck. I could no longer maintain the illusion. I could no longer pretend. I had literally run out of gas. Now I was the one who needed help!

My life had totally fallen apart. I needed my parents and my brother to be there for me. I needed them to listen to me, to care for me, to have my back. Instead they turned their back on me. They chose to ignore me completely and act as if I did not exist.

They literally ceased communication with me. They stopped acknowledging my existence. There are no words. I was shocked to my core. The sadness and grief I went through after that is impossible to describe. I had not known that such depths of suffering were even possible. Now I did.

My recovery took years. I am still recovering from the shock of being rejected and abandoned by my own parents. From a psychological perspective, their insensitive heartless behavior is clearly that of narcissists. Writing this book has been an important and vital part of my healing.

My conclusion is that these shocking new life events were symbolic. They affirm my life's theme of being phony and living a lie. I was being shown what my frightened "little me" had tolerated. I had sold my soul.

I had blindly projected an image of perfection on my parents, my brother and my ex-husband. I imagined that my loved ones loved me as much as I loved them. I lived in what I called my "pink world" of perfect love.

It was a world where there was only love and everybody was happy. It was my way of escaping reality. It was a total fantasy. It was my defense against the terrible truths that I had long suspected yet refused to consider.

I was shattered by the revelation that the wonderful life I had thought I had was all just an illusion. I fought this revelation tooth and nail to no avail. Reality set in and it could not be stopped. I was left with no choice but to let go of my false projections of perfection.

I was forced to see my parents, brother and ex-husband as they really are. My pink love filter was destroyed. I was the only empath in my entire family system! They had no idea what empathy was!

They had taken care of me financially. Yes, I had enjoyed the trappings of wealth. But my total dependence on them even into my forties was their strategy for controlling me.

They had plenty of money. They were multimillionaires. It was easy for them to show their love by buying things for me. But when I needed real love, real warmth, real support, real genuine human sympathy and kindness... they literally walked away and totally dismissed me.

No, I would not be building another Pollyanna story about my perfect family. No, I would not be putting a positive framework around these people ever again. Those days were gone. Life had made sure of that.

I now knew with total certainty that ignoring my true feelings, living a lie and pretending to be something I was not were terrible transgressions. Though I had meant well, I had built my house on shifting sands. When my karma came to collect its debt, that unstable house sank into the convoluted quagmire of naïve self-deception that had been my lifestyle for 43 years.

The life I had struggled for decades to maintain dissolved in front of my eyes in a few short years. It had all been an illusion. It was false. It could not survive the tidal wave of truth that my dream during the year of my awakening had predicted.

I had chosen truth and everything that was false in my life had come crashing down. My awakening was in 2014. My divorce was in 2016.

These dramatic devastating events was all post-awakening. My awakening had been easy. Living my awakening had turned into a living nightmare.

As Adyashanti says in his book *The End of Your World*, "Enlightenment is a destructive process...

It's the complete eradication of everything we imagined to be true."

Fuck one goat!

Insight

Cause and Effect

"Love is the energizing elixir of the universe, the cause and effect of all harmonies."

— Anonymous

My story dramatically illustrates one of life's most important lessons: cause and effect. For every cause there is always an effect. Every word we say and every action we take will always have a corresponding effect.

We are living in the age of Aquarius. This is a time of Truth and of mass awakening on our planet. We now have the opportunity like never before to observe the effects of our actions and thoughts on both an individual and collective level.

It can be frightening to see how many of the collective mass agreements at work in our world were made in fear. This means the consequence will be more fear.

A good question to ask yourself that will help you reflect and move beyond toxic patterns from your past is "What is my motivation?"

Another good question that will help you avoid making the same mistake again is to ask yourself "What would love do now?"

These questions will always create a pause, however brief. In that space we can then make a fresh choice based on truth. Truth always acts with love.

Today the time gap between cause and effect has narrowed and it is getting even shorter. Cause and effect are accelerating. We are seeing almost immediately if not in real time the results of our thoughts and actions.

In the past it took a long time for the effects from our actions to show up. This made the connection between cause and effect more difficult to see.

Nowadays it is easy to follow your causes and see for yourself what you are creating. When you really get this lesson of cause and effect, you will do and say things differently. Then you have learned your lesson. You can move on.

There is always a choice and there is always an effect. The outcome will reflect the nature of the choice that you made. You will finally see that you must take complete and total responsibility for yourself. No one can do that for you. No one else can save you. Only you can do that.

A spiritual awakening greatly quickens this process but it is already in motion. A deep awakening is the fully conscious recognition of this immutable cause and effect process in your own life.

You shed the old false ways and discover how to live as a reborn person. At long last you are free and you know that you are free.

The oneness or unity is now tangible and obvious to you. You will finally understand what love is. You are more than just space. You are love.

You awaken to what is true and what is true has always been true. The truth cannot change. Truth is simple and forever.

It is YOU that changes. You change because you cannot tolerate the false. You quickly let go of any part of yourself that is not being true to YOU!

Ultimately this truth is here and it is now. Realizing this eternal truth that is always here now is just the beginning. You must BE it and LIVE it!

The false is only learned. It is old conditioned or inherited crap that your awakening will automatically discharge with stunning efficiency.

Dump your garbage. Let it all go. You are much greater than that!

Our Abortion

They say when it rains it pours! My post-awakening was a perfect storm!

It was 2017. We were about a year into our affair. I had started working with my partner as a spiritual teacher alongside him. I was also doing one on one session with my own students.

Although both my partner and I were now divorced we were keeping our intimate relationship a secret. The official story was that we were only business partners.

This decision was all mine. I had consulted with a therapist who specializes in working with adolescents plus my own therapist. Both made it very clear that we should keep our affair secret.

I also did my own research. The advice was always the same. Protect the innocent children of divorced parents from any mention of boyfriends or girlfriends while they are healing. I did not want to do any further harm. I kept my mouth shut!

When I began to feel exhausted accompanied by ongoing nausea it did not occur to me that I could be pregnant. I had struggled to get pregnant with my triplets. I was now 44 years old and my partner was 23 years older than me!

Pregnancy was not possible. Having a child was simply not an option.

Eventually I had to admit what my sudden weight gain and my unexplained nausea could mean. We reluctantly bought two pregnancy tests. My partner and I walked to the nearest pharmacy. We purchased them together.

Both showed positive results. The two bright red lines are very hard to miss!

For two people love each other the way we do, my pregnancy was a sudden shockwave of sorrow and joy. Although my partner had not had children with anyone, we were both certain that had we met 20 years earlier we would have had our baby happily.

Now many years later we were not in a place where having a child together was an option. The bittersweet reality was that it was absolutely out of the question.

My abortion took place two weeks later. To my dismay I was even more pregnant than we had thought. My doctor informed me that she was surprised as well.

Any woman who has had to abort knows what this loss feels like. Whether it makes logical sense or not, giving up a little life growing in your body feels like you are giving up a part of yourself. This little life in you is also a beautiful expression of your love for your partner and his love for you. I was truly devastated. We both were.

It worked out that my brother was in town. I had to tell him as I needed a ride to the hospital before and after the surgery. I did not want to raise attention arriving home with my partner. Our relationship was still a secret.

I had to lie to my family and tell them I had some cyst that was benign. It is amazing the lies and bullshit I had resorted to telling. I did not want to disappoint my family. I yearned for their approval as much as ever.

My divorce had already turned into a vicious fight between my father and ex-husband over money. But beyond that I was just scared all the time. I had never felt such fear. Intuitively I knew deep down that my family would never accept Ramaji as my lover.

Although they had accepted him as my business partner, our age gap and our affair would be very uncomfortable for my conservative conventional family. I felt I needed to protect them.

After the abortion I was in enormous emotional pain. I felt confused and empty. I felt like there was a huge black hole in my belly. Yet I did what I had always done in the past. I put a smile on my face and acted the perfect sister/daughter/mother role.

Pretending to be what was expected of me had become a way of life for me a long time ago. But having to hide my abortion and then go on pretending as if everything in my life was just perfect and hunky-dory turned out to be too much for me.

I recognized I could not pretend for a minute longer. Pretending that I did not have deep feelings that I needed to express and acting as if I was invulnerable became intolerable. The truth was that now more than ever I needed the love, empathy and support from my family.

I needed them to step up and reach out to me in my time of crisis. I needed them to be sympathetic and just listen to me and my feelings in a caring way. I needed them to not judge me for my abortion and my love affair with a man 23 years than me.

Yet something told me that if I told them the whole truth now or any time in the future nothing would ever be the same again. As an empath I had long ago begun to feel my family's disapproval. It was a voiceless knowing.

I intuitively knew I could not speak openly to anyone in my immediate family system. Not only had I become a spiritual teacher, I just had an abortion and I was having an ongoing love affair with my business partner.

My family was concerned above all else with their image. Had Ramaji been a billionaire who could invite them onto his yacht, they would have welcomed him and our affair with open arms. Why? Because in their eyes this would have made them look good. They could boast to their friends that their daughter had married one of the richest men in the world!

Even though I knew all of this in my heart, my inner turmoil had reached critical mass. I decided to spill the beans. I decided to tell them everything. For the first time I was going to tell them the bare naked truth. My truth.

The only part I left out was that our affair began before my divorce. I was hoping to maintain at least that drop of dignity.

My revelations were met with cool indifference. There was no sympathy for me. There was no empathy for me. I think my family went into shock.

I told them about my abortion but not about when the actual affair took place or began. I felt that I could still preserve that part of our privacy.

This was not meant to be. I was unable to keep my secret hidden. Eventually my entire family discovered I had lied about the timing.

Two months later my teenagers read my private emails. They sent these private emails detailing our online emotional affair to my ex-husband and to my family. That is when I really began to break down. Life had become more difficult than I had ever imagined possible. My entire life was falling apart.

I had tried so hard to be strong and to deal with the mounting stress on my own. But I now realized that the power of my post-awakening was insisting that I tell the whole truth and nothing but the truth. I felt humiliated yet I could see clearly that I had been dishonest for self-centered reasons.

I had justified my actions by telling myself I was protecting my children and my family. But there was more to it. I was protecting my self-image.

I had sacrificed and compromised and stayed in a loveless lonely marriage so that I could be seen by my children as a good virtuous mother and role model. Now those 16 years of false living and phony image management were backfiring on me. I was protecting their image of me for my own sake.

I believed that I needed their image of me to remain that of a good decent and virtuous woman even if it meant lying to them. I was not being honest with my own self. This is what I mean about the false being exposed. I was being called to tell the truth, live the truth and be the truth.

The unrelenting spiritual power that had been behind my awakening in 2014 was behind this post-awakening process too. My "little I" was fighting to hold onto her "small self" insecure superficial image.

It had been more important to her to *look* like she was virtuous rather than truly *be* virtuous! She needed at all costs to be seen as a virtuous person.

My actions to protect this image were the opposite of virtuous. I was avoiding the truth for my sake not theirs. I was telling lies for my sake not theirs.

Now that I was being honest with myself I could own my mistake.

I was protecting my family in order to preserve their idealized image of me. But that image was based on how I had lived falsely in the past. My error was pretending to be what I thought they needed me to be at the cost of my true self.

Who was I? I was a normal woman in a lonely unhappy marriage who fell deeply in love with another man who got pregnant and had to have an abortion because she already had three incredible smart healthy children.

In the past my need to make a good impression had been so great I did so regardless of the cost. The cost had been my integrity and my happiness. The cost had been teaching my children to be phony instead of authentic.

I could no longer pretend, tell lies or compromise. I began to tell the truth about everything.

My mother verbally insulted me and demonized me at a critical time when my stress was at the maximum and I needed her support more than ever. She knew exactly what was going on in my life at the time. I believe her intention was to get rid of me once and for all.

The seed of her displeasure was my choosing to marry my ex-husband. That was the beginning of what became our irreconcilable split. She felt deep resentment toward me because my father had helped us financially. When I divorced the legal war between my father and my ex disturbed all of us.

I had felt her resentment for many years. It came out in her cruel words any time I needed love and support. I was horrified and shocked at my family's indifference and total lack of empathy.

I could no longer accept it. I could no longer pretend. I was awake.

I had to ask for no contact at this time. I needed space to recover. In my heart I hoped they would recognize and honor how much I was suffering.

I used to visit them at their house three times a week! It should have been obvious to them that I was acting out of character.

My "no contact" request was my cry for help. It was a challenge from me their Eight Challenger daughter. It was meant to provoke a response and initiate a meaningful dialog. After all, they had had 44 years to get to know me!

What happened next shocked me to the core. They jumped on my hothead "no contact" declaration and ran with it. They ceased all contact with me.

It turned out that no contact was exactly what my mother wanted. I believe she planned it ahead of time. She pushed my buttons in expert ways that only a mother who knows their child can do. She shamed me in order to dismiss me. She deliberately provoked me with harsh and cruel statements hoping that I would not be able to take any more and ask for no contact.

As soon as I asked for no contact, the line went dead. My image obsessed family had had enough. They completely ceased communicating with me!

As of this writing they do not answer my texts, emails or phone calls. I'm sure that they feel they have good reason to eliminate me from their family system, ostracize me and pretend that I don't exist.

Since I have made numerous efforts to reach out to them since then, it is obvious to them that I meant for our no contact phase to be temporary.

I remain deeply disappointed in my family. I did not know this type of pain was possible. I had never experienced such total indifference. I never imagined that your own family could turn on you and act as if you are dead.

I learned about narcissism and how it influences the world. It is a lesson I will never forget. It has forced me to understand my empathy and my blind spots like nothing else. My suffering has been my teacher.

These events have been a blessing disguised as a curse. My lessons could not have been learned and integrated without feeling this torment. It is through the no contact that my parents and brother have insisted upon that I was finally able to give up with my false projections on them.

Because they took the no contact to the limit and gave me the classic narcissistic silent treatment, I was forced to let go of my attachments to them. This was an incredibly painful and difficult process. Yet I can thank them for their extreme lack of empathy as it opened my eyes to the truth.

My abortion was physical yet archetypal in its impact. My abortion created a deep need in me to tell the truth. I needed to be heard, to be cared for, to be loved. It was too big and too real. It was too much. I could not lie about my abortion. In a strange way my abortion forced me to claim my new life.

You too will go through an "abortion" where your cherished false ways will need to die. Enlightenment is the death of the false and the birth of the true.

But without the death there can be no rebirth. This death will take place inside of you but it may manifest in dramatic ways in your outer world. If your awakening is deep and real, your life will be rocked by your realization.

As I told Ramaji one beautiful summer day "I could not make this shit up if I tried." Ramaji nodded in agreement. We returned to gazing silently at the serene cloudless blue sky.

Insight

The Stink of Enlightenment

"Enlightenment is ego's ultimate disappointment."

— Chogyam Trungpa

What has astonished me more than anything else since I became a spiritual teacher is the obtuseness of some people who claim to be spiritually awakened. Eventually I sorted out their confusion.

I saw that even after their awakening they were attached to their spiritual ideas and concepts. They were addicted to talking about their knowledge.

They had not let go of their enlightenment. They wanted to stay extraordinary. They were idealizing their enlightened state as being above that of others. Instead of integrating their awakening and moving forward into being an ordinary person, they were stuck on being special.

Staying attached to your awakening is called "the stink of enlightenment" in Zen. It encourages the illusion that an awakened person is "above human." It delays integration. Because the person feels superior, they may fantasize that they are "above the law" and end up doing things that harm others.

Another pattern that left me dumbfounded was how I was being harshly judged by people who thought of themselves as serious spiritual seekers. These were people who knew absolutely nothing about me!

These "spiritual" people were judging me by my looks, by my clothes, by my personality and by what they could see of my home. When they viewed a YouTube clip, they could see my extra high ceilings. I received YouTube posts and emails which boiled down to the belief that I could not possibly be a genuinely awakened person if I lived in a big house or took pride in my appearance!

I had naively thought I could escape this type of person. I had hoped to start my work and be immediately surrounded with like-minded people who were beyond superficial judgments and condemnation based on image.

This was yet another post-awakening lesson that showed the fragments of "hope" that I still clung to. Here again I had a certain belief that I didn't want to let go of.

I believed that spiritual people would behave in a way that made sense to me. I was expecting them to act the way I wanted them to. They did not!

It took me months of dealing with my feelings before I could uproot that righteous belief. In retrospect it was a brilliant test and lesson. It showed me where I was still clinging to prideful views. I was still trying to control others.

I see that spiritual ego or the stink of enlightenment is an enormous problem for our modern spiritual scene. Based on widely spread misinformation, seekers create in their minds an idealized version of what the enlightened person looks like, sounds like and acts like.

This idealized image creates an opening for spiritual teachers to play the role of the "perfect sage." Though they are not intentionally lying to their students, this approach does encourage "spiritual bypassing." Students need to be reminded that their teachers are flawed and very human!

Fortunately, idealizations and limiting beliefs can be dissolved as soon as they are seen. Beliefs are not wrong, just limiting. Limiting beliefs block understanding but the understanding lives on beneath the confusion.

Whenever you believe that your belief is the only right belief you can be sure it is false. Our beliefs are just the thoughts that we have repeated often.

They are not inherently true. Ultimately, they can be traced to the true void.

There the fool's gold of hope dissolves into the sweet serenity of nothingness. There the waves of limiting belief melt seamlessly into a majestic sea of infinity.

There beyond that far horizon we, the lost shining children of heaven, soar joyful as the eagles.

Embrace your humanity. This very world is the Buddha.

I Give Up My Inheritance

Giving up my substantial inheritance was not as hard as it sounds. For me it meant claiming my psychological and emotional freedom.

Although I will forever be grateful to my parents for allowing my family to live in my dad's home and for educating my kids, I have also felt enormous guilt and sadness at the same time. I am a proud woman and when my ex-husband would not help us out financially, my guilt became unbearable.

Working and taking care of myself enables me to return what is not mine. There was so much drama around money during my divorce that it left me with a bitter taste in my mouth.

My guilt and my inner shame around feeling like I was never good enough and somehow had really disappointed my family led to my choice. I could recognize that the time to truly give and be given to is only during life. It is based on being caring and kind. Instead their money somehow felt like a noose around my neck.

I had always been around for my family. I would visit four times a week. I would call daily. My actions were because I wanted to see my parents. I really loved and respected them. They were my best friends. My actions were never about inheriting or needing any money.

It was via my divorce and the way my ex-husband treated my parents and me that created my shame. I did not want to continue taking. I wanted love, acceptance and validation. I wanted them to see the intrinsic value and joy that my new life partner and Twin Flame was bringing to my life.

I needed acceptance after living a life for 17 years knowing that they actively disliked my ex-husband. It was obvious. It created immeasurable pain for me.

My act of disinheritance was only for myself. It was to free my parents of their obvious resentment and allow them the freedom to let me go.

I could now see after meeting my brother's fiancé what they truly wanted. I could not fulfill that need in them. I was not made for that type of person.

I had grown out of my old skin. I was not impressed by the things that used to impress me. I was now thinking my own thoughts. I was feeling all my own feelings. I was a new woman. The girl was gone.

It is, in a strange way, a form of maturity that came over me. I was now able to consciously be the person that I chose to be and walk my talk. I was now able to surround myself with like-minded people who accept me as I am.

Giving up my inheritance was a symbolic and needed action done only for me and about me. I believe that every awakening will lead to the decisive actions needed to embody the awakening in all its newness and fullness.

For me being free means being me. This means I'm allowed my opinions and I'm allowed to live my truth as it is now. I need to live authentically. I want to be treated with the love and respect I give others.

Saying no to my inheritance was the final acknowledgment of what I no longer stand for and the compromises I am no longer willing to make. It is such a relief to know that the people in my life now totally accept me and my opinions and my spiritual inclinations. They love me as I am.

My heartache has shifted into a form of deep self-acceptance. I have an inner knowing about what I will tolerate and what I really can't tolerate.

It is complicated and yet it is very simple. Truth is always simple. Today I live very simply and yet I am happier than ever. To be myself and to be happy is the greatest inheritance of all.

Insight

Never Compromise

"When you are present without the conditioning of your past you become the presence of God."

— Eckhart Tolle

The first thing you realize after awakening is that the need to become enlightened was your ego's need. Your fixation was trying to discover why it feels so phony and out of sorts.

Your higher Self did not need to become enlightened. Your higher Self is already enlightened!

Simply put, you were not clear. You believed you had to get something or go somewhere.

Clarity regarding your own Essence is based on intuitively feeling your connection to your Essence. The key word here is *feeling*.

It is a deep knowing. It is beyond love for knowing your true Self is more important than anything else. When you know your Essence you have this pristine clarity. The clearer you are the higher your LOC!

Often students believe that somehow their skin will change color or they will stand out like luminous heightened sages because they awaken. Bullshit!

You are the same person. You are you. You are more you than ever before. You will feel that being you is completely okay.

The difference will be inside. Your need for applause or recognition for your enlightenment drops away post-awakening. You are deeply humbled. You will delight in being a regular person. You will enjoy life like never before.

This is an area that can deeply frustrate awakened people. You may wonder where your place is in this world. You no longer fit into that familiar little conventional box. Many awakened people have felt that way for months even years.

It may be unrewarding even exhausting when you attempt to share with others the spiritual wisdom you have attained. This is not an accident.

Words do not teach. Your joy, your clarity and your authenticity speak for themselves. Your embodiment of Essence in the form of love, kindness, compassion and the ability to listen will speak volumes. It is a voiceless knowing that you will effortlessly emit to those around you. You will be felt.

In my case, I was literally ignored by many of my nearest and dearest. My need to fit into their world evaporated almost immediately. I quickly found that I was incapable of anything but being totally real and authentic.

The truth was that my life up to that point had often been phony. I had not been real with my own Self. I was not even aware of my own games.

It took a gigantic tidal wave that changed my life beyond recognition to enforce my dedication to truthfulness. Finally I listened to my inner voice.

That was just the beginning. It has taken years of integration post-awakening too. I discovered a wonderful world of pure feeling. I opened up and became vulnerable. The expression "To live life" became "To *feel* life!"

The LOC (Level of Consciousness) of the world population is low. We can see this in the behavior and attitudes of those around us and those in the news.

Love, empathy and sensitivity still run a distant second to money, power and control. People remain indifferent. Most continue to live in a robotic state of consciousness. They still believe that they are their little I. Their fixation runs their show.

Slowly this will shift. The shift is happening now. More and more people are awakening to the fact that as a collective we need to change. This change is internal first. One by one we shift the collective consciousness.

Each one of us makes a massive difference. Perhaps you won't get recognition or applauded but so what! That you live your life as who you really are is what matters. Above all else be true to yourself.

What matters is the love and the joy that you inject into life by being yourself. The results are felt and astonishing. Being yourself is powerful.

Sometimes as an awakened person you are positioned in a city or country that is enmeshed in complex issues and endless problems. You may feel like a fish out of water. This is also no accident.

The city you find yourself living in obviously needs you there. *You* bring the Light that is needed. Not a single thing is an accident. When you start to accept and embrace totally your own Light, then you will *be* the Light.

You will recognize how this intelligence that you are runs this show via synchronicity. You will see how it works in your reality. You become certain!

As a spiritual teacher and your fellow human being, I can feel your Essence. I know immediately how connected or disconnected you are to your Essence.

The way I teach is to challenge your fixations and mirror your truth back to you. This is how I serve you. I challenge your beliefs. I challenge you when you are not being totally honest with yourself. I challenge you in the areas where you are not crystal clear.

I won't ever tell you something you do not know. I am not adding to your treasure trove of intellectual mumbo jumbo. I will not be lecturing you on how to be. I will never discuss consciousness in some bizarre abstract way that only serves to confuse you further.

Instead I will be helping you to awaken from your incessant need to know everything. I am here to help you *un*learn!

My life partner Ramaji and I are dedicated to helping you to live as authentic sensitive beautiful human beings. You are not a robot. You are a unique feeling person who is entitled to be your own true Self in all its glory.

Anything else is a compromise. We do not compromise. We guarantee that you will wake up if you sincerely give us the opportunity to help you do that.

It is your birthright. Claim your freedom. Be your true Self now.

Wealth, Wonder and Awakening

What if my life had been different?

What if my father had never become a multimillionaire?

What if instead of being gone for months on business trips he had worked close to home and spent much more quality time with me and my brother every day?

The wealth never did make me happy.

The opportunity to buy anything I wanted created a never-ending string of countless desires. Buy one expensive designer bag then want another. Snap up one pricey pair of designer shoes then crave a different pair. Get one big beautiful home. Purchase another bigger home with a better location.

Rinse and repeat.

It was just one desire after another. An insatiable flow of endless desires. I won't lie. I enjoyed it. It was a materialistic life. A life spent on the surface.

Let's be clear. I'm not saying that desire is a bad thing. It is a natural force. It is the power of life flowing through us. We exist as human beings because of the desire to BE, the desire to EXIST. Without YOU, what would there be?

We desire the stuff we desire because the people who make money when we buy more stuff have created a consumer culture based not on needs but on more and more desires. Their clever sales manipulations saturate the mass media and social media. Through sheer repetition and a multitude of psychological tricks they convince us that we need that new trendy bag or pair of shoes.

Consumer sheep blindly follow fashion making it a 400 billion dollar global industry. Yet when people fulfill their impulses and own what they yearned for, in that moment there is proof of the ultimate truth.

A brief buzz of satisfaction. A quick thrill of possessing. A short sweet yummy feeling now that your desire is attained. What happens next?

A state of total boredom and emptiness. As soon as your desired is fulfilled, the void appears! It may flicker in and out for only a second. But appear it does. The moment the mind gets what it wants there is a gap. It is a good thing. It is your spaciousness coming forward. Look for it. Don't deny it.

If you are lucky enough to understand the nature of giving and receiving for the sake of sharing instead of for the self alone then your experience will be different and deeper. To receive for the sake of sharing opens you up to natural law, to the circle of life. This is the most efficient method for achieving true happiness.

We are here to receive. Life is giving to us all day every day. The sun, the air, the rain, the food. All just gifts to us. It is how we receive that matters.

To receive in the correct consciousness means we receive so that we may enthusiastically participate in the energetic exchange that is life. The desire to receive is natural. It should not be denied.

Desire is not the problem. Receiving for the sake of self alone stops the cycle of exchange and closes the circle. This robotic consciousness has numbed the western mentality and made it superficial. Surrounded by an abundance of things, we are empty inside. We rarely feel complete and fulfilled.

We live our lives comparing our unique selves to others. We hope for better days. We feel tortured by past deeds. We anguish over lost relationships. All of this is just the mind's way of obscuring what is always here and now!

I get sad when I contemplate how we fail to claim our own power. It is such a joy to relish with pure reverence this amazing reality. Because we can. We can awaken deeply and discover that everything is fresh and new every day.

Then desire is natural. It flows through us like a big happy river. A river of vivid and colorful feeling courses through us all day long. This spontaneous flow of aliveness is the result of an authentic existential spiritual awakening.

Awakening activates our wonder at being a human being. The mental resistance even torment which often tortures human beings gets extinguished.

The ultimate knowing that leads to true peace, love and happiness is something money cannot buy. Knowing this to be true, I must do this work.

My own life has not been easy. It has been filled with a vast variety of rich, sad, bizarre, outrageous and extreme experiences. I did not go off to a cave. I had three children and I lived life to the hilt.

I moved into life not away from it. I experienced the heights that unlimited money can provide. I can honestly say that I know what wealth can offer and what it cannot offer. The true wealth is indeed within.

These experiences led me into my transformation. I had to awaken into the infinite love of I AM! I had to embody my own knowingness. I had to live an authentic existence. It is a life I am very proud to now be living!

Regardless of what I have been through, I do not live in fear or with regret. I live in wonder. The little things turn me on!

If my experience can help anyone, let this be the message it gives.

Let this be the perfume from my life that permeates your consciousness!

It is your birthright to be your true Self. You can awaken and BE HAPPY!

When I woke up from my trance state, I could immediately see the inevitable emptiness that hides inside any form of outer and superficial joy.

That kind of surface joy leaves you if you lose your money, your looks or your power. That image will die one day. It cannot last!

Thank god my spiritual life was mystical!

Thank god for my reluctant awakening!

I had become the very person that I cannot tolerate today.

I was born a deep empath. Yet I was enmeshed in the cloying regalia of wealth. I was fascinated by the dangling baubles of my superficial reality.

My inner world was a tired desolate bone dry desert. Most of my friendships were superficial. Few of my relationships were authentic. Only since my awakening have I had relationships that are honest, real and true.

My life as I knew it changed instantly at the moment of my awakening.

My idea of separation was sucked out of me.

My knowing of truth took over completely and my values shifted radically.

My only remaining big desire was to share my love openly.

To be authentic became the only way I could operate.

Integrity was all that mattered. I could no longer play the old ego games.

I was taken over by a force of my being that had been hiding in my shadow.

I began to peel a huge onion.

Layer after layer of destructive false beliefs were discarded like trash.

The gold was finally found only at the very core of the onion.

At this core there was nothing... and that nothing was everything.

My Self had been lost in the material world.

I could not maintain that illusion. My heart would not tolerate it.

Destructive. That is the best way to describe my awakening!

I am not condemning money. I am not judging wealth.

I love beautiful things, lovely vacations in nature, tasteful comfortable clothing and especially the best high-end makeup!

What I am saying is that it is not a substitute for authenticity. As soon as an "image" becomes your identity, it is then an escape and a distraction.

It becomes a form of narcissism. You live isolated from what is genuine. You ignore what really matters. Something is missing. You do not know reality.

I know this from my own experience.

When money is used to corrupt, control or manipulate, it is a weapon. When money is used wisely with good intentions, it is a great blessing.

The trappings of wealth came at a high price. I believed that my parents would take care of me as long as I pretended to be somebody I was not. I felt that I was not allowed to express myself honestly.

When I spiritually awakened, I found psychological freedom. I could openly express myself. How did my life change? I became completely authentic.

I had felt that they could not tolerate the real me. They could not handle who I really am. When I became outspoken sharing heart-felt truths, it became clear that I was no longer a good investment for them!

I was unwilling and incapable of living a life of compromise. No amount of money, trips, houses or stuff would be enough if it meant I could not express myself and my opinions honestly. Above all else, I had to be me!

If money is used to help and uplift, if it is used in a charitable and genuine way to make a positive difference, it is a precious gift. Money is never the problem. Helping others is not the problem either. When the heart behind the money is open, then money is just another natural energetic flow.

Insight

Knowingness of Beingness

"Nothing is permanent."

— Buddha

Please ask yourself this simple question: "What is the one thing that I know for certain?"

The answer is always the same answer. The one thing that you know for sure is I AM! That you exist is a certainty for you. I AM is a fact.

I call this felt sense that you know that you exist the knowingness of beingness. People know that they exist but they do not investigate it. To know or sense that you exist is only the beginning. It is the tip of the iceberg.

When you explore your sense of existing or feeling of I AM more deeply, you will be led to a subtle experience of your own Presence. It is right here.

Presence is not something you will acquire in the future. You are that now.

Because in non-dual circles Presence is referred to as boundless spacious awareness, spiritual seekers get the idea that Presence is a special experience that they will have in the future. Any moment in which you feel that you exist, that is a taste of Presence.

It is always Here! It is always Now!

Buddhism refers to Presence as Isness or Suchness. Personally, I love the term Isness!

A deeper knowing of certainty in Isness or Presence begins to organically grow in students over time. A gap is revealed. It becomes self-evident that there is a gap between being and thinking.

Meditation can be the catalyst for this. As you get to know your pure beingness separate from thinking, you will begin to realize what an astounding revelation this knowingness of your beingness really is!

Once you have discovered Presence, typically it feels like it comes and goes. You sense it and then you think that you lost it. This is a trick of the mind. You are not losing it. You cannot lose what you are.

When you think you lost Presence what happened is that you identified with your thoughts. You are oscillating between being Presence and being your thinking.

Whenever this identification with thought takes place your Presence is now appearing to you as a thought. You have fallen into *thinking* about Presence instead of *being* Presence. It has not left you. You have left it.

Your identity has temporarily identified itself with a string of thoughts. A string of thoughts is a story. For a few seconds or a few minutes you believe that you are this story. You think that you are these thoughts and that they belong to you.

Do they belong to you? Do you know what you will think next?

No, you don't.

You attract thoughts to you. This attraction is based on your vibration which is in fact what Presence is. It is your individual musical cord. It is your personal vibration.

The more joy and ease you feel, the happier your thoughts will be. You are genuinely happy and therefore you are attracting happy thoughts and happy experiences. This is the limitless power of your focus of attention.

Don't be at the mercy of your negative thoughts. Claim the intrinsic power of your own Presence. Recognize that the only real choice you have is where you place your attention.

Awakening resolves inner struggle. It is the doorway to certainty. The power of Presence eliminates the need for belief, hope or faith. Now you *live* in Presence as Presence. Now you live in certainty.

What is belief? What is faith? What is hope? These are all concepts.

Many spend their lives hoping and praying and clinging to their faith. Yet no amount of this effort produces certainty for them. They are putting the power outside of themselves.

YOU are the Reality!

Do you believe most of the time that you exist but sometimes you doubt it? Did you first have to have faith before you could ever feel that you exist? Are you desperately hoping that you exist but you're still not sure?

Or do you *know* that you exist?

You directly feel and know that you exist. It is a certainty. As a true certainty, it is beyond belief, faith and hope. You do not need to ask for help from an outside power.

Since you are the reality, you are creating your experience. There is no escape from this.

Stability in Presence means living in certainty. You know who and what you are in truth. This is not a belief. It has nothing to do with faith. It is a deep and ecstatic recognition of who and what you really are. To know is to have certainty.

Anything other than this certainty is still missing the mark. To develop this form of certainty takes hard work and courage. It is here right now. But there may be lots of conditioned crap in the way.

This certainty can be described as complete clarity. You prepare your vessel by becoming humble. You purge and discharge whatever stands in the way.

This is the total dedication it takes for a real awakening. You make a total commitment to the truth as you, as your own true Self.

We do not believe the sun shines! We *know* it shines. We don't have hope or faith or merely believe that the sun shines. We don't need those concepts because we have certainty. We have direct knowledge. We know!

You do not have to think about whether the sun is shining or not. You feel the heat of the sun on your skin. The sun is so bright that you can look at it only for seconds. This is the nature of certainty. The mind must step aside.

This is the deepest layer of knowingness. It will come to you during the awakening process. You enjoy security, confidence and inner freedom to a degree you did not know was possible. To be limitless and to comprehend your inner power of Beingness is truly the miracle that waits each seeker.

The Purge

I am trying with my stories to help you understand two things of great significance that happened to me after my unexpected mystical awakenings in 2014. These two things go together. One inevitably follows the other.

These two things do not happen if the awakening is shallow. They will only happen when the awakening is deep.

If the awakening is shallow, then what follows will be superficial. Happy as a a pig in poop, the spiritual narcissist will wallow in the sickeningly sweet stench of his own self-serving enlightenment.

I believe that these two things will take place in any deep authentic existential awakening that is worth having.

They are the Purge and the Peace.

Real awakening is for warriors.

The weak need not apply.

The Purge comes first.

Awakening will be the most destructive event that ever happens in your life. It is not about achieving an ideal state or becoming happier.

It is only about truth! Truth is what I got. Truth about WHAT IS.

My existential truth had to be faced. For what it is worth, the word "destruction" barely begins to describe what took place in my life. Annihilation, devastation, obliteration and extinction will have to do.

Up to the time of my awakening, I had lived a life that for all outward appearances would seem like the perfect ultra-wealthy existence. Homes worth millions of dollars. First class travel wherever we went. Lavish vacations in the lap of luxury at five star hotels around the world.

I had the best cars, clothing, purses and shoes. When I visited my father's company, I was treated like a princess with his employees bowing and scraping before me. My kids were being educated at an exclusive private school. My parents lived up the road. I had many friends and many hobbies.

I should have been happy!

Instead I felt as lonely as a person could be. It is better to be lonely and alone than to be in a phony relationship. The devastatingly empty feeling that goes with being lonely in an inauthentic non-communicative marriage is its own very special kind of hell.

I did not feel love for my husband, the father of my three children. I felt fear. It is hard to describe. He intimidated me. Not only was he a strong athlete and much bigger than me, he would often withdraw, be silent and ignore me. Nothing that I had to say interested him. I did not interest him.

Yet I was accustomed to that behavior. My mother was also an expert at delivering the silent treatment. I felt scared of both my parents as I grew up. I had been taught to hold in my real feelings and pretend.

I had to pretend to be happy even if I was not happy. If I was not acting happy, I was sent to my room. "Come out when you are happy," they said.

The outcome of this treatment was that I felt ashamed. I am a bad person. There is something wrong with me. I married a person who reflected my low self-worth right back at me. He treated me as I was used to being treated.

I was terrified of being myself. Self-judgment reigned. My inner critic ruled.

This negative programming began penetrating deep into my subconscious the day I was born. It continued to control my life with implacable force unabated and uninterrupted up until the very day of my spiritual awakening.

Only then could I begin to clearly see my programming. Even then, even though I could see what had happened to me, I still could not believe it!

This part of awakening is rarely discussed. That really pisses me off. I know it's different for each person. The common fantasy seems to be that there will not be any real issues or painful themes or regular dark human feelings when you wake up. This is the biggest load of crap. It is a spiritual ego trap.

The truth is the OPPOSITE! It becomes impossible to ignore the false within. If there is anything false, anywhere, of any sort, it must go. It will go.

What exactly do you think you are waking up to? A choir of angels singing your glory? No! You are a human being. You were taught to fake it until you make it. Just like me, you were taught to pretend and not tell the truth.

You are waking up to just how full of shit you are.

My story is extreme. My life had to first turn into a living nightmare before I could tell truth from fiction. Every single person that I had placed my faith in turned their back on me. I had to walk on hot coals and get my heart ripped out of my chest before I could see my own projections and introjections.

This was an organic process. It took years. For the first time in my life I allowed myself the time and space to just sit with my own feelings. I allowed myself to feel my vulnerability, my shame, my guilt, my remorse and my pain.

I witnessed the seemingly endless toxic parade of all my past unconscious dark emotions. I didn't just watch them. I relived them. I felt them with my whole body like I never had before.

Because I had suppressed and denied these feelings, there was no other way. They were mine. They were not anybody else's feelings!

You cannot transform hell from a distance. You must get up close and personal. You must be willing to feel it all. You must be willing to die and be reborn. You must allow whatever you were hiding in your shadow to eat you alive.

Thanks to my awakening, I had an eagle's eye view of my every false belief. Layer after layer of pitiful crap emerged. This went on day after day and month after month. I had to face and *live* every feeling I had repressed.

These feelings didn't just come from this lifetime. They seemed to be coming from every lifetime I had ever lived! It was a nonstop avalanche of dark debilitating terrifying emotions. This wholesale elimination of my unfelt feelings took place on a monumental scale beyond my comprehension.

I had no idea what true feelings felt like! The revelation of what true feelings feel like rendered me speechless. I did not know who I was anymore. I swam day and night in a sunless ocean of emotion. Yet I did not drown.

I felt like a helpless butterfly pinned and embedded in an infinite darkness. Yet I did not know that I was a butterfly. Nor was there any hope of ever emerging from this dark void of endless blackness and unbearable pain.

Totally overwhelmed, I gave up all hope. Drunk on poison, I swam in the blood of dying dreams. My tinseltown life had become a house of horrors.

My psychological hell went on for what seemed like forever. I would rock myself back and forth like a madhouse maniac. I cried my guts out. I sobbed from morning until night. It felt so real I thought I was truly going crazy!

An invisible power was scouring me through and through. Every veil of self-deception and every layer of emotional armor was being scrubbed away and permanently excoriated by an immense unstoppable merciless force.

Simultaneously I was seeing my closest relationships with absolute clarity. I was stunned to realize I had lived a lifetime of lies. Lie after shameful lie marched past me in a procession of images I had sought to protect. My slavish devotion to my false, wretched, narcissistic small self was exposed.

I could not get away from this ruthlessly objective x-ray. Not one iota of the new me that was emerging was familiar to me. There was no resemblance!

Where the hell is she? What am I? Who is this?

My parents, my brother, my children, my husband, my friends, everyone who had hated me, dismissed me, judged me and betrayed me... not one of them could cause more harm to me than I was able to cause my own self.

I felt every hurt I had ever inflicted. I lived my life review as if I was already dead while I was still alive. God help me I could not stop this inner torment, not for a single second. It had to be released to set free my own true Self.

The despicable truth about my pathetic ongoing relationships with the narcissists in my life was shown to me. I could no longer deny anything. The comforting veil of my noble gold-plated empathic projections fell away.

I saw with eyes wide open how I had projected goodness and perfection on others while at the same time I took on for them the long toxic shadows that they themselves had denied. My righteous martyrdom sickened me.

Riveted I watched without blinking as my projections of goodness and my introjections of badness fell off me like a haggard old torn T-shirt. Seen clearly, they just dropped away. I was left bare, naked and alone. There was nothing to cover me. Nothing to stand on. There was nothing left to believe.

My projections had sustained me.

Who am I without these projections?

I need my projections!

Month after paralyzing month went by immersed in the pain of my traumatized state. I mourned the loss of my old life. I mourned the loss of my old me.

I mourned the loss of the pseudo-perfect family image I had desperately tried to maintain at the expense of my own happiness. I mourned the loss of my true Self that I had ignored and buried for more than 40 long years.

I grieved. I wept. I screamed. I yearned for peace.

The Peace arrived.

I can say this now.

There were moments when I lay on my bed, red-eyed, surrounded by soggy Kleenex, unable to control my tears, that I would suddenly begin to laugh hysterically. I laughed at my own absurd need to awaken in the first place. I laughed and laughed and man did I wish at those precise moments for the ability to time travel and stop whatever this crazy awakening thing was!

WHY ME?

I wanted the old me back! I wanted the veil! I hated this now!?

This is it? O M G!

Every cell in my body was readjusting itself. I could feel the energy in my physical bones vibrate. I felt my skin tingle. I was a snake frantically shedding its skin. I felt my new skin raw and red under the hot sun.

The truth! This! Raw! Real!

It was months before I could think again or behave in normal human fashion. I would be lying if I did not confess that I almost admitted myself into the nuthouse for observation. I really wanted to do that at times.

Yet miraculously I was able to understand that this — THIS! — was happening in THIS way because this was how THIS had to do it. It was my unique and perfect awakening that simply had to be experienced in THIS way by me!

I did not need to understand it. I cannot conceptualize it. What I know is that I spent years in a bizarre kind of integration that culminated in who I am today. I knew that I had no choice but to fully engage in my NOW. That meant to be with it however it chose to present itself.

I teach many students today. I was teaching at times during this phase too. The Purge enabled me to fully BE with my students in a way I could never have been before all of this happened.

I am filled with love and compassion every day. It is always here!

Ultimately this humbling, destructive and incredibly weird process left me with a capacity to love which is as monstrous as it is glorious! So that I could express and embody truth, the very fabric of my small, false, narcissistic self was transmuted. My ego fixation is not gone. But now it serves truth.

The peace was always here under the surface. It is not the peace that I thought I understood.

The freedom was always here in each moment. It is not the freedom that I had anticipated.

There are no words to describe this freedom and this peace.

Insight

The Shadow

"One does not become enlightened by imagining figures of light, but by making the darkness conscious."

— Carl Gustav Jung

I love this quote because it applies to every one of us. The darkness Jung is referring to is our shadow. Facing this shadow is the hardest part of any awakening and it is the most important.

This does not mean we get lost in our shadows. On the contrary, we get totally lost when we deny that we have a shadow. Our shadows are the parts of ourselves that we are not conscious of.

In my life my shadow areas were numerous, negative and extremely toxic. I was born a deeply sensitive and vulnerable empath. I was raised to pretend that I had no feelings. This meant that I literally did not allow myself to feel any feelings. It meant that my precious vulnerability got locked away in my shadow.

When I was literally forced by my awakening to face my vulnerability, I felt tremendous self-loathing and toxic shame. At first I had no clue where these horrible feelings were coming from. I realized that if I wanted to understand them I would have to allow these feelings to arise without any interference.

It took me months of allowing and feeling these unbearable feelings to purge them. Only then did I reach a point of clarity and awareness where I could let go of my resistance around feeling my pain.

My self-loathing and toxic shame were conditioned into me. They were inherited. They have no place in my big Self. My little I had hid these feelings because I was taught that it was not okay for me to be myself. From birth I had been pretending and acting in order to get the approval I yearned for from my parents.

I now know that I was molded by my parents into becoming a false person. I had become whatever I believed my parents needed me to be in order to make them feel proud of me. I craved their love, approval and respect.

This pattern continued well into my adult life. It was only exposed because of my awakening. I could clearly see now that I was afraid of their judgment and criticism. I was afraid of them.

I was so used to not feeling respected and not being heard that I had become a person I was not. All of this was in my shadow!

As an Enneagram Eight I need to be seen by others as strong. To be honest, as an Eight I had enjoyed being intimidating, bossy and arrogant. These Eight tendencies combined with my parental conditioning to see emotions as a form of weakness turned me into a world class actress.

By understanding and feeling my past issues and recognizing my faults I was able to integrate my own darkness. I could accept it and allow myself to be as I am. I could admit my faults and my fears.

I could now embody the authentic true Self that is me. I was able to fully reclaim my vulnerability.

I am no longer hiding away scared. I am now able to remain open, honest and vulnerable. I am now able to be loving and compassionate. I will always be an Eight, but now I use my considerable energy and my nature as a Challenger to help others go free!

This is how you incorporate your shadows and liberate your true Self. The shadow is only a shadow because it has not been exposed to light. The light is your naturally shining conscious awareness. Bring your conscious awareness into your shadow and it will light up the darkness.

This takes courage. When you finally allow this to happen, your shadow is no longer your darkness. It becomes the brightest Light of all.

We have a collective shadow as well. There are major consequences to hiding in the collective shadow too. Because our collective shadow has been denied for so long, we see many negative things happening in the world.

Recent events are exposing the shadows of our political and economic institutions. The hidden shadowy behavior of famous wealthy political figures is being revealed by a deep purifying force that even they cannot control.

More than ever before, we are now seeing how much was being hidden from us. As shocking as these revelations are, the degree to which we have been lied to by the leaders we trusted is even more disturbing.

Once you begin to see just how deep this rabbit hole really goes, your life will never be the same. Many people still refuse to acknowledge individual and collective darkness. They think it is safer to pretend that things are the way they want them to be rather than look at the way they actually are.

However, they are up against reality. Sooner or later, reality wins. The reality is that we all must come to terms with this darkness, own our truths and make the necessary changes both internally and externally.

To turn a blind eye and bury our heads in the sand, to remain numb and dumb, is the height of narcissism. Evil is not hatred. Evil is indifference.

Each one of us can help. Each one of us has a voice. Each one of us is important. As we bring the light of our conscious awareness into the shadow and take the next obvious baby steps, we will make a massive difference.

When we believe we are small and limited and powerless, we are acting as our little I. If we believe that we are superior, that we know everything and that we are always right, then we are still living in our little I.

When you wake up, you really wake up. You can now see with crystal clarity. Sitting on the sidelines is not an option. Now is the time to take action!

Awakening and the Enneagram

Most books on awakening focus on the journey up to awakening. This book is unique. It is about post-awakening integration.

One of the tools for post-awakening integration that I have found to be incredibly useful is the Enneagram. The Enneagram explains your personality type and "small self" (ego) fixation and how they relate to your big Self.

Why does this matter?

The ego fixation is the main reason that people do not wake up. When you identify which of the nine Enneagram types you are, you can immediately know what your main block to your awakening is. If you are already awakened, then it points to your blind spot and what you must continue to work on.

When you use the Enneagram as a tool for self-inquiry or self-investigation you are quickly able to drill into *why* you react instinctively and why you automatically act, think and feel the way you do. In other words, the Enneagram is a fantastic tool for making the unconscious conscious.

This recognition gives rise to a new way of seeing yourself. You now have a new way of seeing the difference between the Big I and the Little I. The way the little I clings is described by the main fixation of your Enneagram type.

This fixation is the way you preserve your small self. Awakening is not about eliminating your fixation or small self. It is about making your fixation conscious. It is about having spaciousness and choice around your fixation.

When you can turn around and look at your fixation and become conscious of it then you are no longer acting with robotic consciousness. Then awareness shines light on your shadow and reveals your fixation.

Post-awakening we still have bodies and personalities. We still have an Enneagram personality type and that type has its unique fixation.

Typically awakened people have not done much work on their fixation. The tendency is to think "I'm done and now I don't have to work on myself."

They think to themselves "I'm an enlightened person." This is spiritual ego.

Post-awakening is a great opportunity to achieve real clarity regarding your fixation. It is your personality. It serves to differentiate you and separate you.

Just as your body and your looks are unique, your personality is unique. You cannot get rid of your personality even if you try. What you can do is uncover your fixation and make it conscious. Then you are free to see how your small self is operating today and not identify with it. Instead you can laugh at it!

You can see that Enneagram personality types are still fully operational in even the greatest sages. For example, Bhagavan Ramana Maharshi was an Enneagram type Nine. In contrast Nisargadatta Maharaj was an Enneagram type Eight.

Here we have the Nine Peacemaker and the Eight Challenger. Both men were awakened fully! Both were totally being themselves. Yet they had dramatically different personalities.

As a peaceful Nine Ramana embodied the ideal of the serene sage. He sat on his beloved mountain in India wearing a white loin cloth emitting his peaceful vibes to all that were in his presence.

The angry Eight is the Challenger. He challenged his students and shouted at them often. He helped them via his brutal no nonsense honesty.

I use this wisdom to help our students help themselves. By creating awareness around their fixation our students can see how it creates a barrier to their awakening. This clear seeing is freeing.

In my work as a spiritual life coach this clear seeing tends to happen when the student/teacher relationship has organically metamorphosized into a legitimate friendship. Our relationship is then based on authenticity and humility. My students feel free to be their own true and unique Self. They are free to feel their emotions, express themselves and be themselves.

There is no phony posturing at all. It dropped like a false veil. If you are talking about yourself as above or below others then you are not fully awakened. Any attempt to heighten your self-importance based on your awakening is a sure sign that you are not fully integrated.

The measure of true success is itself the ultimate paradox. Your elevation is the knowing that there is nothing to know. It is useless to attempt to describe it. It is not nihilistic. It is the astonishing "not knowing" knowing that a person can have while enmeshed bodily in this human condition.

It is the reason I work so hard. It motivated me write this book. It drives me to serve my students and do my best to undo the many bizarre sacred cows that are misconceptions based on the hopes and speculations of students.

The sages did not intend for misunderstandings like these to occur! Our fragile human egos love to formulate flamboyant misunderstandings based on borrowed concepts and seductive information. After awakening you still work to dissolve limiting ideas.

Your Enneagram fixation serves your monkey mind and your small I. It does not serve your Essence or "Big I" true Self. The nature of the mind is to think, analyze and conceptualize. This leads to idealization.

Idealization means that you turn others or their messages into sacred cow constructs. You act as if the ideas or concepts you have created in your mind are the reality.

You see this very often with gurus and their cults. The follower has idealized the guru into a perfect figure. He can do no wrong. The follower has given all of her power away to this fantasized ideal person.

Many spiritual teachers today subtly encourage a similar top/bottom power dynamic. They pretend to be "above human" and imply that they are abiding in some kind of fantastic perfect state. This is a lie. They are just as human as you and me. But promoting this pipedream to seekers sells tickets!

The mind wants to figure awakening out! The craving for knowledge and the incessant thoughts veil our inner being and block natural intuitive knowing.

My awakening was a direct knowing of this difference between small I and big I. I did not lose my capacity to think. Heaven forbid. Thinking is awesome. It is about letting the mind be a tool. We use this tool. It no longer uses us.

Now I could think for my own Self. Now I was free of inherited and conditioned thoughts that were not mine.

I could now begin living my life totally free or so I thought. I did not understand that I would need years of integration. I did not realize the huge impact my awakening would have on me, on my family and on the direction of my life.

The wisdom of the Enneagram became my go to resource for my post-awakening integration. After studying countless books and learning from many gifted Enneagram experts, I formulated my own unique approach to the Enneagram. I applied it to my own integration. Then I began using my original methodology with my students with great success.

My post-awakening process made me ask questions that I thought I had answered. "Now that I am awakened, why on earth is this suffering happening to me? Why all of these sudden shocks? Why was I still clinging desperately to my projections? How had I not seen this coming?"

I felt driven by a survival mechanism. I felt locked up in chains.

Two full years after my awakening this integration phase became my new path. I was stunned to see just how flawed I really was. For me awakening had been easy. I had believed like so many do that awakening was the end.

What I discovered is that awakening is just a new beginning. Living my awakening has been much more challenging and it never ends.

It has been tremendously helpful to learn about my family's Enneagram types. It speeded up my healing process considerably. I could see clearly that my family members were each a different Enneagram type.

By understanding their Enneagram type I could understand what was driving them. The reasons for their behavior became an open book for me. I took what they did much less personally. I was able to react differently and stop taking on their negative projections.

It has been amazing to me to see this projection mechanism at work in my relationships and then to be able to step free of it. Such insights enable us to feel a deep compassion for others because we can understand their fixation.

My conclusion after years of working with the Enneagram personally and professionally is that the ego fixation or small self is a narcissistic seed that is found in all of us. It is a much needed entity that serves to protect us.

It is our own unique human personality. It is beautiful like a flower. It becomes dangerous only when it decays into malignant or covert narcissism based on selfishness and emotional immaturity. Then the person is incapable of seeing their shadow and owning it. They are obsessed with control and project their shadow on others causing them emotional harm.

People who are interested in self-improvement, emotional healing or spiritual awakening do not develop this toxic narcissism. The toxic narcissist is totally self-absorbed. They have no empathy. They identify with a superficial mask that is glued to the real face.

This mask is their reality. They rely on it for their survival at the cost of their humanity and their true Self. This toxic narcissism in which our empathy for our fellow human beings is lost is a plague on our planet right now.

We as a species are dealing with toxic narcissist tendencies on an individual and collective level. This influence is all around us via the media and other influences on a colossal scale. When you as an individual spiritually awaken and then do your integration work post-awakening, you are doing the very best thing you can do to counteract this modern trend. Your personal awakening takes us one step closer to an awakening of the planet.

Insight

What Is Non-Dual Freedom?

"Enlightenment is intimacy with all things."

— Dogen

Zen makes it very clear. If you try to have a blank mind, if your goal is to be heartless without feelings or emotions, you will become a stone Buddha.

The great Zen master Hui Neng said "If that's your goal, then you might as well be a block of wood or a stone."

To be free or clear does not mean that your thoughts are always pure.

Another great Zen master was asked "What is Buddha nature?"

"A dried turd" he replied.

To be free or clear means that you are free to be whatever arises as it arises. You are one with the flow of life. The stickiness is gone. Thoughts, emotions and body sensations rise and fall like waves. This is life as it is.

Freedom is the ability to just *be* and *feel* what comes up. It is this humble vulnerability and this openness to life itself that is the true definition of awakened freedom. You are so free that you do not need to feel any certain way. Because you are free you are free to feel any state just the way it is.

No posing or posturing. No pretending or hiding. You were born to be yourself. You are entitled to all the rich thoughts, feelings and experiences that life wants to bring you. There is no greater joy than being yourself!

Spiritual seekers confuse this natural spontaneous living in the Now with a state of bliss that is like a psychedelic high. Such states can be experienced but they never last. You will always come back here to this as it is. When you are busy chasing states you are always missing what is right now.

We in the West are very busy. It is normal to have days where you feel overwhelmed. You have bills to pay. You may have a family to take care of.

You work hard and your day is spent running around. This life may not feel like freedom at all. Maybe it feels like shit!

Here is the AHA... So what?

So what if it feels like shit? Who cares? Feel it just the way it comes up!

This is the freedom. It sounds paradoxical. Please give it a try!

Somehow people came to believe that enlightened people do not have bad days or hard times. Many students buy into the myth that awakened people do not have moods or get irritated or jealous or angry or depressed.

Quite the contrary. When a person is pretending that they are above human and always in love and bliss, they are not being true to themselves or honest with us. This is called spiritual bypassing.

I quoted two great Zen masters. Don't be a stone Buddha. Don't aspire to live like a block of wood. Not only that, your dried turds are the Buddha!

The human condition is fraught with internal and external duality. It is the nature of Shakti to experience Herself in myriad ways.

We need the downs to appreciate the ups. We need to know what we do not want in order to explore, experience and know through vivid dramatic contrast what we do want.

To awaken to this truth is the freedom that does not depend on any state.

You just as you are right now are already that.

Regardless of your good or bad mood or what you are thinking or not thinking, your Presence is always right here right now.

Pay attention to the Presence in the background and not to the endless parade of good and bad, beautiful and ugly, likes and dislikes. Sooner or later it will be miraculously shown to you that you via your existential real experience are IT. Right here and right now you are IT and this is IT!

Infinite Precious Value

It was an early morning in August 2019. Several weeks before I had spoken to a relative of mine. I had tried to explain myself to her.

I was yearning to be understood. Her abrupt and cruel indifference after I had expressed myself openly and honestly was the final "aha" I needed regarding my parents and my brother and his new wife.

They had all judged me according to their belief patterns of right and wrong. Deliberately ignoring the sad painful facts of my life, they had knowingly and willingly removed themselves from my life. They did not care or want to know. They could not listen or sympathize. They showed no empathy.

It was after this final attempt to gain understanding that I was able to see their narcissism for what it was. I could no longer make excuses for their cold-hearted behavior.

I know what a kind and loving daughter and sister I was. I had finally come to terms with their inability to reach out or try to understand. They had known the level of my suffering yet decided to eliminate me and dismiss me. I will never be able to make sense of their decision but I could now let it go completely.

This morning in August I asked the universe for a sign. I was accustomed to synchronistic symbols and prophetic dreams from the universe. I was specific. I wanted butterflies. Lots of them.

Later that week, I felt like going out to my backyard to relax in the hot sun. It was then that I saw them.

As if by magic, an orange cascade of what appeared to be hundreds of thousands of butterflies was flying toward me. I was one with them.

They flew around and over the canyon and straight to me. They were a magnificent orange tidal wave. I sat still and smiled as these exquisite monarch butterflies surrounded me on their long migration home.

I stood up and put my arms high up in the air. I closed my eyes and felt the perfection of my Now as they flew by. *This is it* Ananda!

I could feel the freedom of the butterflies everywhere. It was so beautiful. I was mesmerized by this spectacular display of nature's joyful abundance.

Infinite precious value were the words that came to me at that precise moment. I stretched my arms out wide in gratitude. I am free. Now!

These were the words of the late Stephen Jourdain when asked in an interview "What does enlightenment feel like?"

He replied "Everything has infinite precious value!" I cannot say it any better than this.

Today I feel a deep sense of quiet acceptance and a surreal boundless love which is very hard to describe. A stable peace is always here regardless of the circumstances.

I will always love and miss my parents and my brother. I accept their choices. I have learned to let my pain and disappointment go. They will live on as wonderful memories of a love that I yearned for and a projection that I held onto for my survival.

In my heart I know that they do not yet know how to love. I can accept their level of consciousness. It is not up to me. I can allow for their decisions. Even if it hurts like crazy I can move on.

My beautiful children and I are living authentic happy lives. My triplets are my inspiration and my heart. They always were and they always will be. My love is unconditional.

My incredible Twin Flame better half and I love our ordinary life together. We are determined to love each other and to serve and help whoever needs us. This is our mission. Life truly is precious!

With an open heart and a deepened knowing of who I am I can now honestly say that it is not always easy but it is worth it. I survived my awakening in which my life was transformed beyond recognition. Now I am thriving. If I can do it, so can you!

Insight

RASA™ and Levels of Consciousness

"Our purpose here is to recover something that was lost – to return to a part of ourselves that we once had without knowing that we lost it, or when."

— Rav Berg

Imagine the clean clear sparkling windshield of a car. It is so clean and clear that when you get inside the car to drive it, it feels as if the windshield is not even there. You see through it with intense and unpolluted crystal clarity.

After a while this windshield begins to get dirty. It may start off with a little dust. Eventually, after enough time has passed, you cannot see a single thing. It becomes dusty and foggy. Your vision is now totally distorted.

In fact, if you do not clean the windshield, you cannot see through it at all. You can no longer drive your own car!

The totally clear windshield is my analogy for the pure consciousness you have at birth. A baby will spend hours playing with her toes and little fingers. She is not aware of the fact that these are *her* fingers.

She is not yet conscious of herself as a separate person. She is still a part of everything and everyone. Her consciousness is completely crystal clear.

As this baby grows up she learns she has a name. This name is given to her by her parents. By two years old most children have become aware of themselves as a separate individual.

As her parents raise her, she adopts a world view based on her family's world view. Her conditioning begins immediately.

Around age five or six she starts going to school. Now she is learning from her teachers, her friends and her environment as well as her parents. She may already be getting religious conditioning by attending a church, temple or mosque with her parents. She is learning to be civilized.

If she is lucky she will be loved, supported and cared for. If she is extremely lucky she will be taught to ask questions and think for herself. No matter how she is raised, her pure consciousness will get covered with many layers of limited beliefs and inherited conditioning. This does not feel good!

This is when you must take your car to the car wash. Or switch on the windscreen wipers to clean the windshield. You need to get your crystal clear vision back so you can see where you are going and safely drive your car.

This is when the little girl, who is now a young woman, begins to yearn for the clarity that she has lost. Whether she realizes it or not, she wants to return to her natural state. This is when she may begin to look for a teacher.

In my work this is the metaphor I use to describe our spiritual transmission that we call RASA™. It is the car wash. It is the windshield wiper.

The RASA™ spiritual transmission cleans away the dust and dirt in the deep subconscious and accelerates your spiritual awakening. By taking advantage of the RASA™ combined with our expert one on one spiritual coaching, you will find your way back to the natural clarity that is your birthright.

Your LOC (Level of Consciousness) number reflects your clarity. At LOC 1000 (Self-realization) you are crystal clear. Being this clarity is now effortless for you. You live in sahaja, the natural state.

You are clean and clear. You have dealt with your own dirt. You saw it clearly and let it go willingly.

Your conditioning no longer has any negative effect on you.

You are living here/now with incredible lucidity. You enjoy a deep and abiding sense of peaceful well-being. You are completely clean. You are crystal clear about who you are!

The dirt on your windshield symbolizes your resistance and your shadow. That muck and mire on your windshield was in the way of your clear seeing.

As you get RASA™ on a regular basis, you can expect your LOC to go up steadily. When you choose to stay with our coaching and keep getting RASA™, you will eventually reach LOC 1000.

Did your LOC really go up? No, not really. It never had to go up. Your rising LOC is a measure of the fact that you are now living with less and less dust and dirt on your windshield.

Your awareness was always clean, clear and perfect. But you cannot know that when your ability to see reality is blocked and obstructed with all of that subconscious dirt and grime. We help you clean your windshield until its clear. It's that simple!

For some of us, our windshield must first get incredibly dirty before we realize that we are driving blind. Life may force us to clean our windshield!

A spiritual person yearns for her clarity. She knows that something isn't right. She will do whatever it takes. This sincere burning desire is needed in order to awaken.

The gift of RASA™ combined with our online one on one coaching virtually guarantees that you will achieve your spiritual goal. Every person who has stayed on track with us for the required time has achieved enlightenment.

Our mission is to spiritually awaken as many people as possible. We do this work every day. Thanks to our unique affordable proven online process, we have awakened hundreds of men and women around the world.

It brings us great joy to help you help yourself awaken and fulfill your spiritual heart's desire. Once again your windshield will be clear and sparkling. Once again you will enjoy crystal clarity. Finally you will enjoy limitless potential as the divine consciousness which is your birthright!

Appendices

Appendix One

The Heroic Journey of Ananda Devi

Joseph Campbell describes 17 stages of the monomyth or hero's journey (Source: Wikipedia). The hero or heroine lives in the ordinary world and receives a call to go on a great adventure. She is reluctant to follow the call but is helped by a mentor figure.

She then traverses the threshold to the unknown or "special world" where she faces tasks or trials, either alone or with the assistance of helpers.

She eventually reaches "the innermost cave" or the central crisis of her adventure. Here she must undergo "the ordeal" where she overcomes her main obstacle or enemy. She undergoes "apotheosis" and gains her reward (a treasure or "the elixir").

She must then return to the ordinary world with her reward. She may be pursued by the guardians of the special world or she may be reluctant to return. She may need to be rescued or she may be forced to return by intervention from the outside.

Finally, she again crosses over the threshold between the worlds. She returns to the ordinary world with the treasure or elixir she gained which she may now use for the benefit of her fellow human beings. The heroine is herself transformed by the adventure and gains wisdom and spiritual power over both worlds.

My life partner pointed out that there is a direct correspondence between the 17 stages of Campbell's classic hero's journey and my spontaneous path of spiritual awakening. I was quite astonished to hear this. Frankly I don't know what to make of it.

I think having access to this archetypal outline may help you follow the sequence of events before, during and after my awakening. Perhaps Campbell's mythological map will offer you insights when coupled with the modern drama of a mother with triplets.

Here are the 17 stages of the classic monomyth/hero's journey in their exact order as originally presented by Joseph Campbell. I am not saying I am some kind of hero! But the way Campbell's model from ancient history matches my life is a bit shocking to me.

1. The call to adventure... 2. Refusal of the call... 3. Supernatural aid... 4. Crossing the threshold... 5. Belly of the whale... 6. The road of trials... 7. The meeting with the goddess... 8. Woman as temptress... 9. Atonement with the father... 10.

Apotheosis... 11. The ultimate boon... 12. Refusal of the return... 13. The magic flight... 14. Rescue from without... 15. The crossing of the return threshold... 16. Master of two worlds... 17. Freedom to live.

Campbell's 17 Stages Related to Ananda Devi's Life and Awakening

The Call to Adventure

- Her nature as a child: very loving. Kisses homeless people from her car window.
- Has Kundalini experiences as a teenager.
- Sleep paralysis and awake in deep sleep as a teenager.
- Child and teenage spiritual experiences foreshadow what happens in her 40s. Even though she had strong materialistic influences they could not kill her soul.

Refusal of the Call

- Reaction to being awake in deep sleep is panic. She freaks out.
- She is afraid that she is going crazy.
- "I just want to be an ordinary teenager."
- Lives ordinary life. Conforms to parent's expectations.
- Immigrates to USA. Bizarrely, parents follow.
- At late twenties, strong desire to have children. She has wanted to be a mom since she was a little girl.
- She meets an athlete from her home country. They have their culture in common. Strong

healthy genetically superior male. Married in 2000 at 28 years old.

- Gets pregnant with triplets.

Meeting the Mentor

- Kabbalah Centre training.
- Meets meditation guide.
- Her guide has dream of his guru blessing Ananda hand on her head.
- Ananda reads hundreds of non-duality books.

Crossing the Threshold into the Spiritual World

- First Sudden Spontaneous Deep Awakening: Unity (February 2014).
- Meditates all night. It's winter. Wrapped in blankets. Sitting in her movie theatre. Pitch black. Starts with mantra switches to breath meditation. Accessed ultimate void/blackness/bliss.
- Life transformed. Will never be the same. Cannot go back.

Belly of the Whale

- Soon after first awakening, she finds she cannot function normally in her daily life. She goes to a psychiatrist.
- She goes to three spiritual healers. None of this really helps but it is confirmed that she is not going crazy. She is having a desirable spiritual event.
- Second Sudden Spontaneous Deep Awakening: Love (July 2014). While hiking by

herself. New awakening takes her totally by surprise. It turns out to be her life message: "Love Is All. All Is Love."

The Road of Trials

- Profound rage at having been lied to by parents, religion, culture.
- Weeks of writing down false limiting beliefs on paper and burning them in the fireplace in her living room.
- Reaches a temporary welcome neutral state of "no feeling."
- 2015-2016. Recognizing the limitations of this state, she "goes on the road" and attends numerous live group spiritual events in person.
- She insists on meeting one on one with top enlightened teachers many of whom are household names. She is looking for a person who is really living their realization.
- She is looking for an authentic person... not a lover.
- Post-awakening she has become acutely aware of the problems in her marriage. The lack of communication, the indifference, the absence of love, all have become intolerable. She must take action. She has become completely shut down and very sad.

The Meeting with the Goddess (Meeting with True Love or the Soul Mate)

- In her mind her meeting with her life partner Ramaji on February 16, 2016 was just checking out another teacher. In this case one who lived in her area.
- Instead she came face to face with her Twin Flame and the unconditional love that she had always craved yet never received. She knows he is the One literally the moment she meets him.
- What she doesn't know is that in November 2015 Ramaji had a visionary encounter with Kali Ma in which Kali Ma told him directly that his current wife was going to be replaced by a beautiful much younger woman with long dark hair.
- Kali Ma said She was sending her to Ramaji to help him expand his spiritual mission and make it more global. Kali Ma told Ramaji that she is Her "daughter."
- In a future discussion Ramaji shared with Ananda that she looks exactly like the beautiful exotic young woman that Kali had shown him in a mental picture Fall 2015.

The Woman as Temptress (Temptation)

- A massive irresistible force takes her over. She feels tremendous conviction and certainty about what she is doing.
- She falls in love with Ramaji even though they are both married and she has 3 teenagers. Plus he is 23 years older than her.

- She is an artist. Things begin innocently enough with talk about working together on a book cover. Ananda falls ever more deeply in love with Ramaji.
- In April 2016 Ramaji realizes that their relationship is very serious. At this point they are having a full-blown online emotional affair.
- Eventually they meet again in person. That meeting is followed by other physical meetings.
- In late May they make love for the first time. For them both this very special experience is decisive. Their fate is sealed. No turning back now.
- Two weeks later, she tells her husband she wants a divorce. She files for divorce in June 2016.
- Ramaji moves out from his spouse in August. He starts his divorce soon after.
- Committing the sin of adultery is the rupture or violation of a taboo that sets in motion a dramatic process of emotional cleansing and life level purging.
- Her extreme action violates her original heartfelt vow to be faithful to her husband, yet she is being honest with herself. Something is terribly wrong with her life.
- Her awakening is now going to a deeper level of her Being. Like a house of cards in a strong gust of wind, her life will come

crashing down. Her life will be changed until it is unrecognizable.

- She has succumbed to temptation and "fallen from grace." At the same time it is an authentic response to the undeniable call to embody her awakening.
- The body is asserting itself. This call of the flesh is a bold step into aliveness and real living. Liberating her erotic second chakra is key to her emotional healing.
- She enters into an authentic Tantric awakening and transformational process. There is no real awakening of the emotional without the awakening of the sexual.
- That her affair climaxes in sexual love union is a necessary evil. It sets in motion the required destructive force that quickly brings her family system of mother, father, brother and ex-husband crashing down around her. It is the trigger.
- She had been living in a deep empath "Pink World" of escapist fantasy. Its failure was long overdue. She had been living a lie for far too long. The truth will come out.
- Enlightenment is the most destructive event. Everything that is false falls away. A life lived in truth replaces it.
- Her children discover the detailed emails of their online romance.

Atonement with the Father (Entering the Abyss or Facing the Most Powerful People in Your Life)

- She is insulted and maligned by her ex in ways so extreme you cannot imagine.
- Confrontation with her biological father, her mother and her husband. This series of confrontations begins with her divorce.
- She becomes pregnant and has an abortion which only increases the stress and sadness.
- Stacking up of events leading to final crisis and confrontation. Her mother proclaims "You have demons. Your brother's fiancé is an angel. Nothing like you."
- Shocked to her core, she systematically disconnects all strings tying her to her family. She asks for "No Contact" in order to take a break from all the madness.
- Her parents turn on her and use her request to their advantage. They give her the Silent Treatment. This means they totally stop responding to her. No emails, no texts, no phone calls. It is as if their one and only daughter doesn't even exist!
- She is subjected to extraordinary psychological and verbal abuse.
- Everyone in her family system turns on her. Though she had been deeply embedded in her family system and loved them dearly, all is dismantled. The bridge has been burned. They refuse to acknowledge her. She cannot go back.
- A legal war erupts between her ex-husband and her father. She and her kids are the victims. The ex-husband doesn't care about

the harm to her and her children. All he cares about is getting a settlement from her father.

- Her father comes to the house and says "Your kids will know the truth!" They will know that their multimillionaire grandfather was always their parent, not Ananda? Ananda's 17 years as a devoted wife and loving dutiful mother and daughter amount to nothing?

Apotheosis (Death, Transformation and Rebirth as a New Empowered Person)

- She goes "No Contact" after her mother's "demon" comment. To her shock and dismay, they welcome this arrangement. They do not contact her again.
- This includes her father who she always thought would have her back.
- Her "Pink World" of perfect love is destroyed. Annihilation takes place.
- She finally recognizes that her toxic shame and guilt and "I'm not good enough and I will never be good enough" self-image are not natural. She was raised to believe that something is wrong with her. She is the black sheep.
- Darkest of the dark: confusion, grief, meaningless, powerlessness, sadness. Indescribable endless sadness. Day after day is filled with non-stop crying.
- Total paralysis. Bed ridden. Falling apart. No hope. The seven levels of hell.

- Very intense very difficult healing journey of recovery with no end in sight.
- Her pregnancy precipitates physical transformation. She gains weight.
- Death of her assumptions, projections and introjections. Now her personal energy goes to feeling completely all the feelings she had denied.
- Her consciousness is devoted to knowing, experiencing and expressing reality as it is. She is the last woman standing. She accepts what is.
- She was phony, a hypocrite and just acting before in order to please her parents and survive under their financial control. She is reborn with a brand new way of life ahead of her.
- She understands how being a deep empath led her to live for others and utterly neglect her own needs. She has no idea what she likes or needs or wants!

The Ultimate Boon

- At last she is her own person. She is no longer a mental/emotional slave for anyone. She is no longer being shut down by her ex-husband. The price for this psychological freedom and wholeness is enormous. There was no other way.
- Ananda becomes a spiritual teacher. She starts awakening people. Her Eightness

makes her highly effective. She achieves big results quickly with lots of people.

- She did not know that following her two spontaneous deep awakenings there would be such massive changes to her psyche and to her external life. None of the books she read said anything about it.
- The destructiveness of enlightenment and the absolute demand post-awakening to be authentic and embody the oneness and love that was recognized in her awakening dominate. This becomes her message due to the dramatic and extraordinary events in her life.
- Many spiritual teachers are content to ramble on about "resting in the Absolute" or "abiding in the Self." It is obvious that they have not taken responsibility for the final act of the spiritual journey: the all-important return to the world and to authentic ordinariness. After what she has experienced, there will be no more BS!
- She realizes her natural style is Zen. By now she has helped many students awaken. Her emphasis on being totally ordinary and fully embracing her natural feelings with the whole body while being a mother is echoed by Zen.
- According to Zen full integration of a major awakening takes 7 years.
- Real enlightenment is total destruction. You are not enlightened. You are not spiritual.

You are not superior. Let it go! It is just spiritual ego. It is just narcissism.

■ Evidence says the embodiment sequence of awakening is from head to heart then life. It drops from mental body to emotional body to life body (prana & physical). It goes from thought to feeling to physical body to dramatic obvious manifestation in external life.

■ Awakening opens the mind. Love opens the heart. They are separate tracks but they both need to be opened and integrated.

Refusal of the Return

■ Ramaji suggests that she write a spiritual autobiography to support her spiritual teacher career.

■ She wants to write a book but she is extremely private.

■ She strongly resists the idea.

The Magic Flight

■ Ananda and Ramaji go to Europe in May 2019.

■ They give satsang in Munich, Germany and meet with students. The trip is utterly magical.

■ The time away on this successful work vacation sends a powerful message to her family that she is moving on with her new life independent of them.

- This trip was a powerful affirmation of her future. It was like a vision quest. Now they have started celebrating their new life together. It was an incredible trip!

Rescue from Without

- Ananda is being true to herself. There is no error. It is necessary for her to focus internally at this stage of her healing journey.
- She starts writing furiously about her life, her break from her parents and everything she needs to say that will end up in her *Intimacy with the Infinite* book. She gets external help as needed.
- Ananda needs help to complete her task of making "the elixir" available to the public. This outside help comes to her because she is doing the right thing.
- It is a humbling experience for her to ask for help but that also makes it the right thing for her as she writes from her deepest inner truth.

The Crossing of the Return Threshold (to the New or Reborn Ordinary World)

- She returns to the ordinary world as a regenerated and accomplished being.
- The heroine has gone through a wonderful and terrible journey.
- Writing and publishing a book about her journey is her heroic proof that she has returned.

Master of Two Worlds

- She is now the master of two worlds: both ordinary and enlightened.
- At the same time, she has transcended both and integrated both.
- Now she is simply ordinary. She is not enlightened. She is just being herself.
- She has successfully articulated her unique true message. She has brought back the elixir of authentic freedom united with real love.
- She shares generously and joyfully as she awakens people and changes lives.
- Her life has been transformed beyond recognition from a fake and phony fear-based existence to a triumphant declaration of her unique authentic loving true Self.

Freedom to Live

- This journey of mastery and unfolding is never ending.
- There is the event of real enlightenment and there is a before and after due to that event.
- She is now a free and liberated Being.
- She is more deeply and completely human than ever before.
- She will continue to work on herself to become more authentic and more loving.
- She is a boon to mankind. She humbly aspires to share her spiritual wealth with as many people as will receive it. She enjoys the peace beyond understanding.

Appendix Two

Ananda Devi, Natural Born Zen Master

Please allow me, Ramaji, to apologize in advance. I need to set the stage for Ananda Devi. I think that some students may assess Ananda based just on appearances. She is young and beautiful. She speaks with an elegant accent. She has a powerful warm personality. She awakened spontaneously.

The first edition of *1000* was finished and published in 2014. It was the culmination of three years of intense productivity during which I wrote and published eight books.

After *1000* was published, no more books showed up to be written. These books had come to me one right after the other begging to be written. The process was entirely spontaneous. In essence, these books truly wrote themselves.

My three-year writing frenzy finished, I found that I was faced with some tough truths. My marriage was not really working. I was not happy. I was now in a new chapter of my life. In the cold clear light of a new day, I now could see that my prolonged fit of workaholic productivity had also served as a distraction from what had become painfully obvious: my marriage was dead.

Fast forward about a year to November 2015. I experienced a vision from Kali Ma. She spoke to me briefly and very directly as is Her style. I remember now and will always remember her blunt words: "Soon your wife will be gone. She is being phased out. I am sending you someone to replace her. She is My daughter. She will assist you in spreading RASA to the world."

Kali Ma showed me a picture of her. She had long dark brown hair. She was beautiful in an exotic way that appealed to me profoundly. Furthermore, the image She showed me reminded me of my favorite poster of Kali Ma from India.

Kali Ma concluded by saying "She will appear to you shortly. You do not have long to wait."

Coincidentally, I had already set up a phone consultation with Jerry, my spiritual psychic friend in Canada. 2019 Update: Jerry has told me that he is no longer offering intuitive sessions. However, in 2015 he was still giving consultations.

As we approached the conclusion of this November 2015 session, Jerry lowered his voice in a dramatic fashion. "I have something to say but it may shock you. I need your permission in advance."

I replied "Of course I want to hear it! Please proceed."

He then said "I have to tell you that you will no longer be in your marriage. This takes place in 2016. There is someone else coming into your life who will replace her. She is quite a bit younger than you."

I nodded my head and said "Go on. Thank you for being direct. I am not surprised by this."

By November 2015 I had already decided that I needed to get a divorce and move on. I was crystal clear about this. I just didn't know how to do it. But I knew Kali would show me the way. More likely than not She would do so dramatically and decisively! There would be no looking back!

He concluded the session with words of caution. They came out slowly with pauses in between. He was deeply concerned. "However... I must warn you... she will be very Kaliesque!"

I laughed. "Jerry, you are incredibly accurate as usual. Kali contacted me two months ago. She said the same thing!"

What did Jerry mean when he said Ananda would be very "Kaliesque"?

For those of you familiar with the Enneagram, Ananda Devi is an Enneagram type 8 wing 7. The Kali archetype is that of a passionately loving woman whose fierce true universal love is dedicated to the rapid authentic spiritual awakening of as many people as possible as quickly as possible.

It is that of an Enneagram type 8 wing 7 woman. As one of Ananda's students recently put it, reflecting what many have said of her: "Ananda Devi is the most real authentic loving and fierce woman I have ever met."

In the early afternoon on February 16, 2016, Ananda Devi arrived to get a session with me and receive RASA™. The moment I opened the door and saw her I knew there was something very special about her.

During our session, I told her that she would be brilliant at teaching non-duality. I knew this like I know the sky is blue. Over the years I have told a few students they would be a good non-dual spiritual teacher, but not in the first session!

It was clear that she was already deeply awakened. She was at LOC 1000. But I did sense that she lacked integration.

In retrospect, I should have immediately suspected that she was the woman Kali was sending me. But somehow a veil was kept over my eyes for several months. An online romance developed.

By June, we had both decided that we needed to move on from our respective marriages. We both immediately got divorced. I trained her to be a RASA™ giver. She began giving satsang with me in January 2017.

Ananda Devi is 23 years my junior. At the time of this writing (June 2019), she just turned 46 and I am 68 (until September). This radical age difference is common among Twin Flame unions. It is impossible to describe our relationship as there is nothing to compare it to. It is as if I had never really had a real relationship before.

I had been looking for a certain special someone since I was 16 years old. At long last I had found her. I had finally found the love of my life.

An Enneagram Type Eight, she is fiery, forceful, passionate, confrontational and refreshingly direct. In my opinion, Kali Ma is also Enneagram 8. The dynamic, warmly outgoing and delightfully provocative personality of Ananda perfectly matches what was predicted about her by both Kali Ma and the remarkable spiritual intuitive Jerry of Canada. Sadly, as of 2019, he has decided to no longer offer his unique services.

At the same time, Ananda is the single mother of three teenagers. In fact, they are triplets! She is incredibly warm, caring and compassionate with a heart as big as the sky. When she works with a student, she invests her total heart and being into their awakening and integration. She cares deeply and profoundly for them. She literally fights for them!

She has many times helped sick and ailing students for free. She is much more generous and willing to help others than I am. I am more impersonal and businesslike. I am glad that she is willing to act like a universal mother on behalf of those who are suffering. It does not come naturally to me to do that.

Her students range from wealthy businessmen to single mothers to therapists to other spiritual teachers. They all find her uniquely direct approach a breath of fresh air. Ananda loves to kill sacred cows. She fiercely embodies authenticity and expects the same from her students. She naturally speaks in a Zen style based purely on the intensity of the moment.

I would like to shift gears and talk about Ananda's background more from her perspective. Many people think it is easy to be an effective spiritual teacher who awakens people into non-duality. In fact, what we do is one of the hardest jobs in the world.

Although she had already had incredible mystical experiences which made her understanding rock solid, I spent much of our first year working together helping her to recognize this incredible gift she was born with. I knew it was her destiny. I had known this with an unshakable certainty from the day I met her. I had tremendous faith in her ability to guide and awaken others. That faith has never wavered.

She moved on from her old life to join spiritual forces with me with her head up high. She is a woman of tremendous courage. My respect for her grows daily. Every day I am more impressed by her.

She complements me in many ways. For example, she cares deeply about what happens to people post-1000. It seems to me we are very much like mother and father. She wants to make sure our post-1000 students ("spiritual children leaving the nest") are going to be okay. In contrast, my attitude is that if they got to LOC 1000, then they will be fine. Time to move onto the next person and help them go free!

She and I often share students. If somebody is stuck, then it is common for us to send the stuck student to the co-teacher. In practice, though, here is what really happens!

People rarely if ever get stuck with Ananda! But they can and do get stuck with me! A typical scenario is that a student might get stuck working with me. I send this student to Ananda. They then quickly go up in LOC and rapidly finish!

In other words, even though I could not get the student to LOC 1000, Ananda Devi is able to do so rapidly, reliably and with incredible efficiency. She is a natural spiritual genius.

What does this mean? As much as it pains me to say it, Ananda Devi is better at coaching people and getting students to LOC 1000 (Self-realization) than I am!

Like me, she does her coaching in conjunction with giving RASA™. Furthermore, she has developed her own unique approach to spiritual life coaching that uses the brilliant Enneagram system to easily diagnose spiritual blind spots.

Her compassionately confrontational yet very warm and personable style gets to the root of student issues in record time. She truly is a natural at this very difficult and demanding profession. She has personally awakened more than 100 students. She has finished every single person I sent to her.

In fact, she complains to me that she finishes people too quickly! Yet this is her purpose: to finish and awaken as many people as possible as quickly as possible on this planet now!

We live in exceptional times. We live in a time of global awakening. We live in a time when the life-giving love power of woman, of the Shakti, of the Goddess, of the Divine Feminine, needs to come forward and proclaim Her power.

Ananda Devi is just such a woman. She is a natural born leader. Strong, courageous, unquestionably feminine, a devoted mother, she embraces this path with all of her heart.

Frankly, any human being who has the golden opportunity to work with Ananda will be tremendously blessed. She is the most extraordinary human being I have ever personally known. She is a tremendously gifted master teacher. Her heart is huge and made of solid gold. She is truly a gift to the world.

I would like to add that my own life has been totally renewed, recharged and uplifted by her presence. She has challenged me in many ways that have enabled me to break through limitations and ceilings I did not even know I had.

When Ananda Devi entered my life a new chapter began for me. Just as predicted by Kali Ma, Ananda Devi has played a major role in expanding the reach of RASA™ throughout the world. She is responsible for training new RASA™ givers. Thanks to her we created a new California corporation Rasa Transmission International, Inc.

She has provided the impetus to turn my little old "mom and pop" business into a global platform fully prepared to reach as many thousands as are ready for the RASA™ spiritual transmission shaktipat breakthrough for rapid spiritual awakening. Thanks to her, we are ready for global awakening.

At RasaTransmissionInternational.com, you will be presented with the opportunity to work with me or to work with Ananda Devi. I have spilled the secret that Ananda Devi is in fact better at coaching and awakening people than I am.

While it is true that I wrote the *1000* book, please understand that Ananda Devi is in my opinion the most naturally gifted spiritual life coach and awakening agent for enlightenment on the planet today. Not only that, she will make your journey of awakening fun, exciting and enjoyable even at its most challenging. Remember, I go to her when I need help!

I do not want you to miss out on the opportunity of working with her. Please remember that I have been "working" with her since February 2016. She has transformed me and my life in wonderful and fantastic ways! I am stunned by her positive impact and blown away by how effective she has been at helping me see and transform my weaknesses and blind spots.

Frankly, I thought major positive changes like this were impossible or nearly so at my age and stage. Yet she has reached into me and rejuvenated and awakened me far beyond what I had hoped for or expected. I submit to you that you too will be blessed, elevated and transformed by your sacred association with this new and brightest star in the modern spiritual teacher firmament.

Love and Blessings,

Ramaji

Appendix Three

2019 RASA™ Satsang European Tour

Ramaji and Ananda Devi in Austria

All Day RASA™ Satsang Event with Ramaji and
Ananda Devi May 18, 2019 in Munich, Germany
With Our German Translators Gunnar and Patrick

Appendix Four

RASA™ with Ananda Devi and Ramaji

Don't miss out! There is nothing else like the RASA™ spiritual transmission. It is a unique spiritual opportunity like no other.

If you are already in non-duality (600s or 700s) then getting to LOC 1000 (final liberation) could take you only 3 months.

If you are starting out in the 560s, 570s or 580s, then please allow 6 to 12 months. That's right. You can be enlightened (achieve stable Self-realization) in just one year or less.

We have succeeded with more than 500 people around the world. We have dozens of testimonies from satisfied seekers who finally achieved their spiritual Goal.

Our timetable assumes that you have two one on one online RASA™ coaching sessions per month from the comfort of your own home or office. Anybody with a good job can afford our sessions.

We coach and integrate you along the way in conjunction with Enneagram insights and other unique strategies designed to reveal your blind spots and effortlessly clear subconscious blocks to awakening. The RASA™ spiritual transmission does the rest!

No need to go to India and live in an ashram... become a monk or nun... or go on grueling 10 day Vipassana retreats.

No need to take a week's vacation from your job and save for that $5,000 (travel, event cost, room and board) luxury non-duality retreat with yoga, vegetarian lunches, new age music and awakened teachers who put you to sleep when they talk.

We make it easy and affordable for you to work with us. Not only is our approach simple, easy, no nonsense and down to earth, it is fast, affordable and totally transparent.

To be in non-duality (600s to 900s) is not enough. Only LOC 1000 (Self-realization) will bring an end to lifetimes of seeking.

Yes, the spiritual technology now exists to effortlessly accelerate and virtually guarantee your awakening and Self-realization. Think of the RASA™ as a "spiritual Internet download." We live in a time of fast results!

All we ask is that you be honest, earnest and have a Burning Desire to Wake Up... NOW!

Just give us a chance. We are not just spiritual "teachers." We are finishers! If you work with us, you WILL get to LOC 1000!

No More Seeking!

Take the Leap!

Get RASA™ Today!

Appendix Five

How to Contact Ananda Devi

To Sign Up for Ananda Devi's Free Monthly Newsletter:

https://www.rasatransmissioninternational.com/

To Contact Ananda Devi:

satsangwithananda AT gmail Dot Com

To Contact Ramaji:

satsangwithramaji AT gmail Dot Com

Our Website:

https://www.rasatransmissioninternational.com/

To Book a Live Online RASA™ One on One Coaching Session with Ananda or Ramaji:

https://www.rasatransmissioninternational.com/book-your-session

Ramaji and Ananda Devi YouTube Channel (Features interviews plus free recorded online Zoom Satsangs with group RASA™ given in the last 20 minutes of the event):

https://www.youtube.com/channel/UC4gwdyNdE9VfR9tazFiqKFA

Video Interviews & Video Testimonials from Our Students:

https://www.rasatransmissioninternational.com/testimonials

https://www.rasatransmissioninternational.com/media-kit

Thank You!

Love Always,

Ananda Devi

Made in the USA
Las Vegas, NV
08 June 2024

90858946R00174